SPPU New Syllabus

A Book of

HISTORY

EARLY INDIA : POST MAURYAN AGE TO THE RASHTRAKUTAS

for

First Year B. A. (Semester - II)
New Syllabus as per CBCS Pattern,
June 2019

MISS RUPALI KULKARNI
M.A., History, SET
Pune.

NIRALI PRAKASHAN
ADVANCEMENT OF KNOWLEDGE

N5146

History Early India : Post ... **ISBN 978-93-89686-38-8**

First Edition : November 2019

Published By:
NIRALI PRAKASHAN
Abhyudaya Pragati, 1312, Shivaji Nagar
Off J.M. Road, PUNE – 411005
Tel - (020) 25512336/37/39, Fax - (020) 25511379
Email : niralipune@pragationline.com

➤ DISTRIBUTION CENTRES

PUNE

Nirali Prakashan (For orders within Pune) : 119, Budhwar Peth, Jogeshwari Mandir Lane, Pune 411002, Maharashtra, Tel : (020) 2445 2044, Mobile : 9657703145
Email : niralilocal@pragationline.com

Nirali Prakashan (For orders outside Pune) : S. No. 28/27, Dhayari, Near Asian College Pune 411041
Tel : (020) 24690204; Mobile : 9657703143
Email : bookorder@pragationline.com

MUMBAI

Nirali Prakashan : 385, S.V.P. Road, Rasdhara Co-op. Hsg. Society Ltd., Girgaum, Mumbai 400004, Maharashtra;
Mobile : 9320129587 Tel : (022) 2385 6339 / 2386 9976,
Fax : (022) 2386 9976
Email : niralimumbai@pragationline.com

➤ DISTRIBUTION BRANCHES

JALGAON

Nirali Prakashan : 34, V. V. Golani Market, Navi Peth, Jalgaon 425001, Maharashtra, Tel : (0257) 222 0395, Mob : 94234 91860;
Email : niralijalgaon@pragationline.com

KOLHAPUR

Nirali Prakashan : New Mahadvar Road, Kedar Plaza, 1st Floor Opp. IDBI Bank, Kolhapur 416 012, Maharashtra. Mob : 9850046155;
Email : niralikolhapur@pragationline.com

NAGPUR

Nirali Prakashan : Above Maratha Mandir, Shop No. 3, First Floor, Rani Jhanshi Square, Sitabuldi, Nagpur 440012, Maharashtra
Tel : (0712) 254 7129;
Email : niralinagpur@pragationline.com

DELHI

Nirali Prakashan : 4593/15, Basement, Agarwal Lane, Ansari Road, Daryaganj Near Times of India Building, New Delhi 110002
Mob : 08505972553, Email : niralidelhi@pragationline.com

BENGALURU

Nirali Prakashan : Maitri Ground Floor, Jaya Apartments, No. 99, 6th Cross, 6th Main, Malleswaram, Bengaluru 560003, Karnataka;
Mob : 9449043034
Email: niralibangalore@pragationline.com

Other Branches : Hyderabad, Chennai

niralipune@pragationline.com | www.pragationline.com

Also find us on f www.facebook.com/niralibooks

Preface ...

I take great pleasure in presenting this book of "***History***" to the students of F.Y.B.A. (Semester – II) of the University of Pune. This book has been written in accordance with the new syllabus w.e.f. June, 2019. The history of Early India is a crucial part of Indian history. It is a base for understanding the entire Indian History.

It helps the students to understand the history of Early India from Mauryan Age to the Rashtrakutas. This book highlight the culture of India along with the dynastic history of India. This book will help the students to understand the contribution of early Indians to polity, art, literature, philosophy, religion and science and technology. It also aims to foster the spirit of enquiry among the students by studying the major developments in early Indian history.

I express my sincere thanks to ***Mr. Dineshbhai Furia*** and ***Mr. Jignesh Furia*** of Nirali Prakashan, Pune for having published this book. A special thanks to ***Mr. Prasad Chintakindi, Mr. Ravindra Walodare, Mrs. Sarika Supekar*** for their valuable contribution to this book.

Any suggestions from students and teachers for further improvement of this book shall be welcome.

PUNE **AUTHOR**

November 2019

✿ ✿ ✿

Syllabus ...

(New Syllabus from June 2019)

F.Y.B.A. – SEMESTER – II

HISTORY

Unit 1 : CENTRAL ASIAN CONTACTS AND THE AGE OF THE SHUNG - SATVAHANAS

(a) *The Indo – Greeks, theShakas, the Parthians, the Kushanas: Economy, Society, Religion and Culture*

(b) *The Age of Shung – Satvahanas : Polity and Administration, Society, Economy, Culture*

Unit 2 : EARLY HISTORY OF SOUTH INDIA

(a) *Period of Sangam Literature – Society and Culture. Early Polities*

(b) *Economy : Towns, Trade and Crafts*

Unit 3 : NORTH INDIA : GUPTA AND HARSHVARDHAN

(a) *The Gupta Empire – Brief Political History, Administration, Society, Trade, Science and Technology*

(b) *Harshvardhan : Administration, Religion, Education*

Unit 4 : REGIONAL KINGDOMS : A BRIEF HISTORY

(a) *The Chalukyas, Pallavas, Pandya – Struggle for Supremacy over Peninsular India*

(b) *Rashtrakutas, Palas, Parmaras – Tripartite Struggle*

(c) *Literature, Religion, Art and Architecture*

✿ ✿ ✿

Contents ...

✿ ✿ ✿

UNIT – 1

CENTRAL ASIAN CONTACTS AND THE AGE OF THE SHUNG - SATVAHANAS

SYNOPSIS

1.1 Central Asian Contacts

1.1.1 The Indo - Greeks

The most important event after the fall of the Mauryan Empire was the attack of foreigners from the North-West. The unguarded north-Western frontier attracted Greeks. After Alexander, a large portion of his empire came under the rule of his generals. The two principal regions were Bactria and the adjoining regions of Iran known as Parthia. In about 250 B.C. Diodotus, the governor of Bactria revolted against the Greeks and declared his independence. Some important Indo-Greek kings were Euthydemus, Demetrius, Eucratides and Menander. Demetrius son of Euthydemus passed further into India.

Among all the Indo-Greek rulers Menander (165-145 B.C.) was the most famous. He reached Patliputra. He ruled for almost twenty years. He gave stability to Greek power in India. His capital was Sakala (Modern Sialkot) in Pakistan. Greek writers gave information that he was a great ruler and his territory extended from Afghanistan to Uttar Pradesh in the east and Gujarat in the west. This Indo-Greek king is best known as Milinda as a Buddhist text refers to him in Milindapanho. Menander was converted to Buddhism by a Buddhist monk Nagasena. Menander asked Nagasena many questions related to philosophy and Buddhism which together with Nagasena's answers are recorded in Milindapanho or the questions of Milinda.

In the history of India, the Indo-Greek rulers are the first ones whose coins carried the portraits of kings and their names. The Indo-Greeks were also the first rulers who issued gold coins. The Indo-Greek coins are known for the depiction of realistic and artistic portraits.

The portrait of the king on the obverse side appear to be real portraits. On the reverse some deity is depicted. It is through the coins alone that we come to know more about than forty Indo-Greek rulers.

1.1.2 The Shakas

The Indo-Greek kingdom in India did not last long. Due to disturb bances in central Asia the Scythians or the Shakas a nomadic tribe attacked Bactria and later invaded the Greek kingdom in India and controlled a much larger part of India than had the Greeks. There were five branches of the shakas with their seats of power in different parts of India and Afghanistan. One branch settled in Afghanistan. The second branch settled in Punjab with Taxila as its capital. The third branch settled in Mathura where they ruled for about two centuries. The fourth in Maharashtra and Saurashtra where the shakas continued to rule until the fourth century, and the fifth in central India with Ujjain as its capital. The Shakas ruled in different areas from the first century B.C. to about fourth century A.D.

Although the Sakas ruled in different areas of the country, only those who ruled in Central and Western India rose to prominence.

The most important ruler of western India was Nahapana whose mention is found in various inscriptions found in Maharashtra and in the records of the Satvahanas. The rule of Nahapana was full of events. There were wars, expeditions and charitable benefactions of the central Indian branch. The most famous ruler was Rudradaman. It looks like that his rule extended over a vast dominion including the areas of Gujarat, Sindh, Malwa, Saurashtra, North Kokan and parts of Rajasthan. The Shakas in these regions benefited from the seaborne trade in Gujarat and issued numerous silver coins. Rudradaman is famous in history because of the repairs he undertook to improve the Sudarshana lake dam when it was damaged by heavy rains. This dam was used for irrigation for a long time and dated back to the Mauryas. Ujjaini the capital of Rudradaman, became a center of culture and education. He was a great lover of Sanskrit and issued the first - ever long inscription in Chaste Sanskrit. Many historians think that Saka Era was founded by the Sakas. In about A. D. 390 the dynasty came to an end with the defeat of the last king at the hands of Chandragupta II of the Gupta dynasty.

1.1.3 The Parthians

Shaka domination in North-Western India was followed by that of the Parthians. Parthians also known as Pahlavas were Iranian people from where they moved to India. In comparison to the Greeks and the Shakas they occupied only a small part of north-western India in the first century A. D. The most famous Parthian king was Gondophernes during whose rule St. Thomas is said to have come to India to propagate Christianity. He ruled from A. D. 19-45. Soon after Gondophernes, the Parthians rule in India ended and the Kushanas came into power. Excavations at Begram in Afghanistan have brought to light a large number of coins of Gondophernes, but none of his successors.

1.1.4 The Kushanas : Economy, Society, Religion and Culture

Rise of the Kushanas :

The Chinese historians tell us that the Kushanas were a section of the Yueh-Chi race. The Yueh-Chi were a nomadic tribe settled on north-western border of China. In the year 165 B. C. they came in conflict with a neighbouring barbarian tribe known as Hiung-nu. The Yueh-Chi were defeated by the Hiung-nu and forced to move out of their land. They could not move towards the east since the China wall had become a barrier. They had no option but to move west and south. While moving Westward the Yueh-Chi came in conflict with another tribe called Wu-Sun whom they defeated easily. At this time the Yueh-chi were divided into two sections. Those Yueh-Chi who settled. On the border of Tibet came to be known as the little Yueh-Chi and those Yueh-Chi who continued the westward came to be known as the Great Yueh -Chi which finally came to India.

After Wu-sun the next people Yueh-chi met were the Sakas who occupied the territory of Bactria. The Sakas tried to defend themselves against Yueh-Chi but were defeated by them. The Saka's were forced to leave their land and they came to India and the Yueh - Chi settled down in the land of the Sakas. It is here that they gave up their nomadic life and adopted an agricultural and a settled way of life. Further possibly, in this area great Yueh-Chi were divided into five branches.

Kadphises I :

According to Chinese sources, the first great Yueh-Chi king was Kujula Kadphises also known as Kadphises I who united all the five groups. He also adopted the title of Wang or king. He also invaded and captured the kingdom of Parthia, Kabul and Gandhara. He also consolidated his power in Bactria. The Indo-Greek and Indo-Persia rulers were completely defeated in the time of Kadphises I. He called himself 'great king'. He is also called Dharmathida and Sachadharmathida (steadfast in true faith) which is taken to suggest that he was Buddhist. Kadphises I issued copper coins and probably no gold coins. Kadphises I died at the age of 80.

Kadphises II :

Kadphises I was succeeded by his son Wema Kadphises or Kadphises II who extended the Kushana territory upto Punjab and a considerable part of the Gangetic valley probably as far as Banaras. Kadphises II issued extensive gold and copper coins and is referred to as great king and a devotee of Shiva. On some of his coins Shiva holding a trident and bull are shown. Kadphises II was not only an able king, but also ruled over a vast empire.

Character and Achievements of Kanishka :

Kanishka was the greatest of the Kushana emperors. Infact Kanishka is undoubtedly the most striking figure among the Kushana kings of India. "A great conqueror, a patron of Buddhism, he combined in himself the military ability of Chandragupta Maurya and the religious zeal of Ashoka". Kanishka is usually regarded the successor of Wema kadphises. There is no unanimity among scholars regarding the date of Kanishka's accession to the throne, but the most accepted date of his accession to the throne is 78 A. D. Some historians think that Kanishka founded the Saka era.

Conquests of Kanishka :

Kanishka was a warrior. Like Samudragupta and Akbar, he too believed in the policy of aggression and aggrandizement. By the valour of his arm he not only marked victories in India but also in countries abroad. When Kanishka came to the throne, his empire comprised of Afghanistan, a larger part of Sindh, portions of Parthia, Bactria and the Punjab. He extended the limit of his empire by the following conquests.

Wars of Kanishka :

Kashmir : Kanishka conquered and annexed Kashmir to his empire. However we do not have any details of his war with the ruler of Kashmir. Many towns, gardens and ruins of the buildings belonging to the reign of Kanishka survive even upto this day. Kanishkapura, a city after the name of Kanishka was also founded by him in Kashmir.

War against the Saka Satraps : The Saka satraps of Northern India were sufficiently powerful upto the reign of kanishka. Kanishka defeated the saka satraps of Punjab, Mathura and Ujjain etc. the Saka ruler most probably was chashtan. The result of this war was that Sakas acknowledged the supremacy of Kanishka and ceded certain portions of Malwa to him.

War against China : Kanishka was responsible for the conquest of Khotan, Kashgar and Yarkand. Kanishka not only defeated the Chinese, but also demanded the surrender of hostages.

The capital of this vast empire of kanishka was Purushapur i.e. modern Peshawar. Coins of Kanishka had been found from almost all over the above mentioned area.

Kanishka and Buddhism :

Kanishka's reign also marks a turning point in the history of Buddhism and Buddhist literature. It witnessed the rise of Mahayana Buddhism and the magnificent literacy activity started by Parsva, Asvaghosa, Vasumitra, Nagarjuna and others. It was during Kanishka reign and mainly through his efforts that Buddhism was successfully introduced into central and eastern Asia. It is true that Kanishka became a Buddhist but that does not mean that he became intolerant towards other religions. We find Kanishka worshipped Surya. He respected all other religions as it is shown by his coins which bear images of gods worshipped by the Greeks, Persians and Indians.

This is in keeping with the tradition of complete freedom and toleration in religious faith which is the marked characteristic of Indian culture as a whole.

Propagation of Buddhism :

After his conversion to Buddhism, he channelized his energy to the propagation of Buddhism. The best example of this was the convection of the fourth Buddhist council. The council was convened at Jalandhara according to certain authorities while others hold the view that it was met at Kashmir. The chief purpose of the council was the complication of the doctrines of Buddhism and writing of commentaries on them. The whole of the Buddhist literature was thoroughly examined. Voluminous commentaries on the three Pitakas were also prepared. Most of the comments were collected in a book known as Mahavibhasha. The old Hinayana form of Buddhism was replaced by a new form of religion that is Mahayana. The fourth Buddhist council which was called by Kanishka was attended by about 500 monks including Vasumitra, Asvaghosha, Parshwa and Nagarjuna. According to the Sarvasvati school of Buddhism Kanishka summoned this council at the instigation of an old and learned monk named Parshwa. Vasumitra acted as the president of the council while Asvaghoshah as the vice-president.

Propagation in Foreign Countries :

Like Ashoka Kanishka, also sent missions abroad. Missions were sent to China, Japan, Tibet and Central Asia and in these regions Buddhism attained popularity.

Transformation of Buddhism : In the Kushana age Buddhism in its new form spread rapidly to many countries beyound the borders of India Mahayanism is called the northern school with pali as the medium of its sacred texts.

Steps for the Spread of Buddhism :

Many old monasteries were repaired and many new ones were also built. A lot of money was distributed among the Buddhist monks for their maintenance. A large number of stupas were set up in the memory of the Buddha.

Patron of Art and Learning :

Kanishka was a great patron of art and learning. Large quantities of sanskrit literature of high standard both religious and secular were created during the rule of Kanishka. His name is familiar with various Buddhist writers namely Asvaghosha, Nagarjuna, Vasumitra and Charak. Ashvaghosha was a versatile genius well versed in music, literature, religion philosophy and debt. Buddhacharita, Saundaranan-da Kavya, Vajrasuchi, Satriputra prakarna are important among his works including a number of other works. Buddhacharita is a complete life of Buddha written in the form of Mahakavya. This is considered to be the epic of the Buddhists. Another great figure of the court of Kanishka was Nagarjuna. He was not only a great teacher and philosopher but also a scientist. He was famous of one of the most important exponents for Mahayana philosophy. His best work is prajana Paramita Surasastra. Nagarjuna enunciated the theory of relativity in his great work called Madhyamika Sutra. Vasumitra a leading Buddhist theologist was the writer of Mahavibhashya Sastra, which gives us volumes of information on Buddhist philosophy. Another illluminary of Karishka's court was Charak. He was the well known writer of the great book called Susruta and 'Charaksamhita' on medicine. Mathara, a politician of rare intelligence was a minister of Kanishka. These and other important personalities like the Greek engineer Agesilaus "played a major role in the artistic, religious, literary, scientific and philosophical activities of the reign". Taxila and

Mathura emerged as great centres of art and culture during Kanishka's reign.

Kushanas Administration : The kushana administrative system contained some foreign elements along with some indigenous one. The most important foreign element was government by Satraps who were viceroys or Governors of the provinces. Some functionaries had foreign names Strategos for a general or military Governor Meridach for District Magistrate. There were also officers of Indian designation such as Amatyas and Mahasenapati (Commander-in-chief) While the former officers were functioning in the North-West the latter were in the interior. Kingship was the prevailing type of polity, although there are mention to republics also. The Kushana rulers gave themselves high sounding titles like Kaiser, Devaputra and Shahi-sahanushahi etc. There was a strange system of two kings ruling at the same time during the Kushana period. Satraps in India were called Kshatrapas and Mahakshatrapas who were practically independent kings. The term "Dandanayaka" and "Maha Dandanayaka" occur for the first time in the Kushana records. The Kushanas were the first to introduce this system which was later on followed by the Guptas. the empire was divided inot smaller administrative units callsd (1) Rashtra, (2) Ahara, (3) Janapada, (4) Dera or Vishaya.

Buildings of Kanishka :

Kanishka was a great builder. His important buildings and works of art are found in Kanishkapura, Peshawar, Mathura and Taxila. He erected various buildings and Kanishkapura in Kashmir. Peshawar was the capital of his kingdom. Kanishka adorned his capital with many noble edifices, public buildings and Buddhist monasteries. Various buildings belonging to his reign are found in Peshawar. The most important monument of Kanishka in Peshawar is a relic tower of bronze called shah-ji-ki-dheri. This multi - storeyed relic tower enshrining the relics of the Buddha. The Chinese traveller Hieun Tsang who came to India in Harshvarshan's period has written about this stupa. The most important sculpture from Mathura is the headless statue of Kanishka. The city also had a large number of statues, sculptures and monasteries. It is also believed that Sirsukh city of Taxila with all-its hall, monasteries and buildings was found by Kanishka.

Coinage :

We have a large number of coins of the Kushana period. Kanishaka, Huvishka and Vasudeva issued gold and copper coins. They did not issue any silver coins. An interesting feature of the Kushana coinage is that the figure of the various deities worshipped by the different people living in the Kushana Empire. It is important to note that images of the deities from countries like Iran, Bactria and other neighbouring religions are also found on the Kushana. The name of the deities figuring on the coins of the Kushana rulers are many.

The Kushana coins were inspired by the ideals of both Buddhism and Brahmanism. A study of the Kushana coins proves that the Kushana empire was equally the empire of the Brahmanas as that of the Buddhists.

Estimate of Kanishka :

Kanishka is undoubtedly the most striking figure among the Kushana kings of India and also one of the greatest kings of ancient India. He was a great warrior, a great empire builder a great patron of art and learning. No Indian king has ruled over such a huge empire in central Asia as was done by Kanishka. It is not sursprising that Kanishka occupied a unique place in the history of India. Kanishka was not only a great conqueror, but also a great administrator. It is important to note that there was not a single revolt during his rule.

Downfall of the Kushana Empire :

Kanishka ruled from A.D. 78-101 After him came Vasishka, Huvishka, Vasudeva and others. The decline of Kushana power set in after Vasishka, though the Kushanas continued to rule up to the fourth century A. D. over small principalities independently under some sovereign kings.

Economic Condition :

The most striking feature of the post Mauryan period is the thriving trade between India and the western world. With the improvement of the internal communication by the Mauryas, the construction of highways gave impetus to the internal trade. The conquest of north-west India by the West Asian powers promoted closer contacts with Western and central Asia. The Kushans controlled the silk route which started from china and passed through their empire in central Asia and Afghanistan to Iran and Western Asia which formed part of the Roman empire in the eastern Mediterranean zone. The Indian merchants participated as intermediaries in the Chinese silk trade. Central Asia acted as a link between India and China with the emergence of Roman empire as a permanent power the western world started trade with India and became the chief customer of its luxury goods. This led to the increase of money economy and coins were used for trade. As this route was a source of substantial income for the kushans they built a large prosperous empire on the strength of the tolls levied from traders. In the north West India the Kushanas circulated the copper coins it is also important to note that the kushans were the first rulers in India to issue gold coins on a wide scale.

The Kushan as also encouraged agriculture. The earliest archaeological evidence of large - scale irrigation in Afghanistan, Pakistan and Western central Asia date to the Kushana period. In creased commercial activity and consequent growth of money economy led to a proliferation of arts and crafts leading to greater specialisations and to the achievements of greater technical skills in certain spheres of production. The influx of Chinese silks into India stimulated the silk industry here. Increase in trade demanded an efficient organisation of production and distribution. The individual artists got together and formed guilds and the merchants also organised themselves into corporations. The guild system became a general pattern of production, facilitating high output. In the Mathura region and Western Deccan Inscriptions attest the existence of many. These guilds sometimes acted like the banks. The membership of the guild provided social status and security to the artisans.

There were sea faring merchants. A safe return from the sea was a happy event in the life of a merchant. Workers in metals included blacksmiths, coppersmiths, goldsmiths, needle makers, workers in tin, iron, ivory, brass, workers in glass and lead etc.

Social Life :

Society was divided not on the basis of wealth or profession, but on the basis of birth. There are mention of marriages in the same caste between members following different professions and of varying status, but there is no reference to inter - caste marriage. The four caste mentioned are the Brahamanas, Kahatriyas, Vaishyas and the Sudras. Brahmanas occupied a position of privilege and were held in high esteem.

The Greeks, the shakas, the parthians and the kushans eventually lost their identity in India and in the course of time becoming completely Indianized. As most of them came as conquerors they were absorbed in Indian society as a warrior class that is as Kshatriyas. They came to be considered second class Kshatriyas. The foreigners were assimilated into Indian society on such a large scale in no other period of ancient Indian history as they were in post - Mauryan period.

Religion and Culture :

Some rulers and others from central Asia adopted Vaishnavism. While a few other rulers adopted Buddhism. The famous Greek ruler Menander became Buddhist. The questions and the answers that he exchanged with the Buddhist teacher Nagasena is a good source for the intellectual history of the post - Maurya period. It was during the Kushana period that Mahayanism made its presence and the Buddhist religion was divided into two parts. Kanishka summoned the fourth Buddhist council to settle the Buddhist doctrines. But in general the Kushans followed a policy of religious intoleration. Brahmanism. Buddhism and Jainism flourished side by side. The deities found on the coins of the kushana rulers are not only Brahmanical and Buddhist but also Greek, Mithraic, Elamite, Sumerian and Zoroastrian deities. The Kushana rulers did not make their personal religion the religion of the state. Kadphises II was a follower of Siva, Kanishka was a follower of Buddhism. Vasudeva was a follower of Siva.

Gandhara and Mathura Schools of Art :

Gandhara Art : In the north-west developed the hybrid Indo-Greek form of art where though the themes were Indian, the depiction was heavily influenced by western art. It is popularly known as Gandara School of art. The Kushana period is famous for the growth of Gandhara art. The Gandhara School portrayed entirely Buddhist themes. In Gandhara art stucco was a popular medium and the monasteries of Afghanistan were decorated with lots of stucco images. The images of Buddha in different positions and sizes were produced by the Gandhara artists. One of the finest examples of the Gandhara art is the big statue of Buddha at Bamiyan. The most important centres of the Gandhara school were at Hadda, Bamiyan, Jalalabad, the swatvalley and the Peshawar district.

Mathura Art :

The Mathura school of art also flourished during the Kushana period. To some extent mathura art was influenced by the contemporary Gandhara school. The Mathura school has the distinction of having produced the first image of the Buddha. This school also produced many fine specimens of sculptures that include images of Jain, Buddhist and Brahmanical deities and the life size sculptures of Yakshas, Yakshini and portraits of kings. This school is not only famous for producing the headless erect statue of Kanishka whose name is inscribed at its lower end, but also produced several stone images of Vardhamana Mahavira. The examples of the Mathura art are found at Mathura, Sarnath, Begram, Kausambi and Saheth Maheth.

The images of the Mathura school were made of red standstone from sikri. They show traces of yellow and white but the spots were hidden on account of the fact that the entire surface was covered with a paint.

1.2 The Age of the Shung - Satvahanas

1.2.1 The Age of the Shung - Satvahanas

Shung :

The Mauryas were succeeded by the Sungas and they ruled for 112 years from 187 B.C. to 75 B.C. It is said that Pushyamitra the army chief of Maurya king Brihadratha, killed the king while the latter was reviewing the army. It is pointed out that the army did not revolt against Pushyamitra proves that it was loyal to the commander than to the king. Pushyamitra maintained the title of Senapati only even after becoming the king.

Origin of Sungas :

Tradition describes the Sungas as Brahmans of Bhardwaj gotra who occupied a high position.

History of Sungas :

As already has been mentioned pushyamitra, the founder of Sunga dynasty was the commander-in-chief of Brihadratha the last of the Mauryan kings. The success of Pushyamitra it so appears was due to the general feeling of dissatisfaction against the weak Mauryan rulers who failed to protect the kingdom against the adventurous Greek invaders who seem to have advanced without any hindrance to the very outskirts of the imperial capital Patliputra.

Pushyamitra Sunga :

Pushyamitra proved himself to be an able and powerful ruler. Soon after having risen to power he endeavoured to strengthen the shattered and weak kingdom of Magadha. It was during his rule that his son Agnimitra conquered Vidarbha. The ruler of Vidarbha was Yajnasena a relative of a minister in the Mauryan court. He declared himself independent after the usurpation of the Magadhan throne by Pushyamitra. Agnimitra defeated Yajnasena Vidarbha was captured and brought back to the fold of the empire Pushyamitra is said to have suffered a reverse from Kharvela, the king of Kalinga though it cannot be proved convincingly. Pushyamitra had to face an invasion of the Yavanas also. It is said that after reducing Saketa, Mathura and Panchala, Yavanas reached upto Pataliputra. We do not know much about this war. But we also do know from literature that Pushyamitra Sunga performed Ashvamedha after this war. Pushyamitra also assumed the title of 'Chakravarty' in commemoration of these sacrifices indicates a period of continuous peace, prosperity and success. The sacrificial horse was guarded by Vasumitra, the grandson of Pushyamitra. Further Malvikagnimitram, mentions of the defeat of Yavanas on the bank of river Sindhu at the hands of Vasumitra. The empire of Pushyamitra was much smaller that that of the Mauryas. Buddhist tradition depicts Pushyamitra as a great persecutor of Buddhism. But this allegation does not seem to be true because there is a definite mention of a donation to the stupa at sanchi and Bharhut during the rule of Pushuyamitra. According to the puranas Pushyamitra ruled for 36 years.

Successors of Pushyamitra :

Pushyamitra was succeeded by Agnimitra in about 148 B.C. From Kalidasa's drama Malvikagnimitram we learn that Agnimitra had been the governor of Vidisa during his father's reign and had gained experience in statecraft as governor of Vidisa. He ruled for about eight years. No events of his reign are known. There are no inscriptions or coins of his reign. Agnimitra was succeeded by Jethamitra, and after him came on the throne Vasumitra, son of Agnimitra. During the rule of his grandfather Pushyamitra he had won laurels in the battle against the Greeks when commanding the forces escorting the sacrificial horses let loose by his grandfather. After his accession to the throne he does not seem to have kept up the martial spirit and vigour of his youthful days. He buried himself in the lap of luxury. From Bana we learn that he was very found of music and dancing and was killed by Muladeva or Mitradeva while enjoying a concert. The puranas talk of ten kings of the Sunga dynasty. The ninth important king of this dynasty was Bhagavata and in whose court Heliodorus the ambassador of Antialkidas stayed. The last king of this dynasty was Devabhuti.

According to purnas, he was an incapable and ease loving ruler. He was put to death by his Minister or Amatya called Vasudeva Kanva. Thus the kingdom of Magadha was passed from the Shungas to Kanvas. After the rule of the Sungas, Kanvas came to the throne.

Extent of Shunga Empire :

The Empire of Shunga was half to that of Ashoka. Their empire extended from the Sutlej in the east to the river Narmada in the South. In the West the empire extended upto the modern Sindh.

Importance of the Shungas :

In the history of India the Shunga dynasty occupies a very important and enviable place. Their greatest achievement was to safeguard India from the invasion of the Hunas. They valiantly resisted the attacks of the Hunas and saved India from being destroyed. They contributed a lot to the development of culture also. This dynasty infact ushered in a glourious era in the annals of Indian history. The shunga kings greatly encouraged the Brahman religion and literature. Besides religion and literature art too received a fillip during Shunga period Patanjali's Mahabhasya throws light on it. The

Sanchi and Bharhut stupa of this period stand testimony to the fact that architecture, painting and other arts developed during this period and reached the acme of their glory.

Satvahanas :

While northern India was reeling under upheaval after the fall of Mauryas, a very mighty kingdom was established by the Satvahanas also known as Andhras in parts of Andhra Pradesh and Maharashtra.

Simuka to Satakarni II :

Simuka was the founder of the Satvahana dynasty and he ruled from 235 B.C. to 213 B.C. He was succeeded by his brother Krishna. During the tenure of his rule he continued a policy of conquest. The third king was Satakarni I who seems to have made extensive conquests and performed two Ashvamedha sacrifices and one Rajasuya sacrifice. We have a lot of useful information from an inscription of his queen Nayanika as his achievements are described in detail in the Nanaghat inscription. It appears that he conquered Western Malwa, Vidarbha and Ahupa. He took up the title of Dakhinapathapati. His name also occurs on one of the gateways of the Sanchi Stupa. Substantial donations were made by the Satvahanas for the renovation and decoration of Sanchi Stupas and monasteries. It is possible that Satakarni I was killed in the battle-field. The next important king was Gautamiputra Satakarni. In between three kings ruled of whom Satakarni II ruled for about 56 years. During his reign Malwa was conquered by from a successor of Pushyamitrasunga. After Satakarni II the expansion of Satvahana empire received a blow and Nahapana appears to have won part of Satvahana territory. A large number of coins of Nahapana have been found in the Nasik region.

Hala :

The next important name of the Satvahana dynasty was Hala. He was the 17th king of the line. It is said that king Hala was the greatest king in peace. He was a poet king. He wrote a great poetical work Gathasaptasati in Prakrit.

Gautamiputra Satakarni :

The Satvahanas became powerful again during the rule of Gautamiputra satakarni. He was the most outstanding monarch of the Satvahana dynasty. His achievements are recorded in glowing terms in the Nasik inscription of Queen - mother Gautami Balasri. He has been described as the destroyer of the Sakas, Yavanas and Pahlavas. He overthrew Nahapana and restructed large number of his silver coins. He also recovered northern Maharashtra, Konkan, Vidarbha, Malwa and Saurashtra form the Sakas. The boundaries of the territory under his direct control extended form the Krishna in the south to Malwa and Kathiawar in the North and from Berar in the East to the Konkan in the West. He took up the title of Tri-Samudra-toya-pita-vahana. Gautamiputra Satakarni is the first king bearing a metronym and this practice was followed by nearly all his successors.

Vasisthiputra Sri Pulmavi :

Gautamiputra was succeeded by his son Vasisthiputra Sripulmavi in about A.D. 130 and ruled for about twenty four years. The coins and inscriptions of Vasisthiputra Sripulmavi have been found in Andhra Pradesh. This shows that by the middle of the second century, this area had become a part of the Satavahana kingdom. He set up his capital at Pratishthan (Modern Paithan) on the Godavari river in Aurangabad district. The Sakas resumed their conflict with the Satvahanas for the possession of the Konkan coast and Malwa. The Satvahanas were defeated twice by the Saka ruler Rudradaman, but he did not destroy Satvahanas fully on account of matrimonial relations.

Sri Yajna Satakarni :

Possibly, Sri Yajna Satakarni was the last of the great Satvahana rulers. He recovered North Konkan and Malwa from the Saka rulers. His inscriptions have been found in Andhra Pradesh and coins form Gujarat, Maharashtra, Andhra Pradesh and Madhya Pradesh. His love for navigation and overseas trade and activities is shown by the representation of a ship with a fish and conch on his coins.

The successors of Yajna were, weak and unworthy to rule over such a large regime. They ruled over small territories. The Satvahana empire broke down when Abhiras captured down Maharashtra and Pallavas and Ikshvakus conquered the eastern region.

The Deccan during the Satvahana period :

On the basis of the information derived form coins, literature and inscriptions of the Satvahana period. We can have an idea of the political, social, religious and economic life of the people.

Social organisation :

The Satvahanas originally seems to have been a tribe of the Deccan. But they were Brahmanised and their most famous king Gautamiputra Satakarni claims to have established the four-fold varna system which had fallen into disorder. The Satvahanas were also the first rulers to make land grant to the brahmanas. The Satvahanas show traces of a matrilineal social structure. It was customary for their kings to be named after his mother. Such names as Gautamiputra and Vashishthiputra proves that in their society the mother enjoyed a great deal of importance. Sometime queens acted as regents. The best examples of it was queen Nayanika. But the Satvahana ruling family was basically patriarchal because succession to the throne passed to the male member. While the Maharathis, Mahabhoja Satvahana society was divided into four classes. The first class consisted of the Mahasenapatis. They formed the highest class in the society. The second class consisted of both officials and non-officials. Among the officials were Amatyas, Mahamatras and Bhandagarikas. To the non-official class belonged the Naigama (merchant), the Sresthin (head of a trade guild) and the sarthavaha (head of a caravan of traders). The third class belonged the tribe, cultivator, carpenter, fisherman, physician, druggist, goldsmiths, blacksmiths and gardener.

Srenis : Srenis or craft guilds were a normal feature of the Satvahana period. The prevalence of these guilds shows that the institutions of self-government were common in the country. The srenis were not only craft or trade guilds. They acted also as banks. Money could be deposited in those guilds and that money carried interest very often endowments were made to the srenis because guilds were considered to be more permanent than an empire which could be destroyed at any time. Whenever investments were made interest was paid on them. The rate of interest varied sometimes it was a percent and sometimes 12 percent per annum.

Foreign trade : During the satvahana period foreign trade and commerce flourished. The Deccan played an important part in the commercial relations of India with the west paithan and Tagara were important marts of those days. The most important harbours were Sopara and Kalyana. The satvahanas did not ignore the development of the marine. Trade and colonization must have been helped by peace and progress in the country Royal encouragement must have played its part. The Roman demand for articles of luxury must have been responsible for commercial activity.

Currency : The currency of the country consisted of Karshapana which were both silver and copper Suvarna a gold coin was equal to 35 silver Karshapanas. One Karshapana weighted 146.4 grains and one Ratti was equal to 1.83 grains.

Religion : As the religious conditions of the people during the Satvahana period both Hinduism and Buddhism flourished side by side. The Satvahana kings were Brahmans and from the very beginning kings and queens performed the vedic sacrifices such as Ashvamedha, Vajapeya and Rajasuya. They also worshipped a large number of vaishnava gods such as Krishna, Vasudeva and others. Not only sacrifices were performed a lot of money was given to the Brahmans as Dakshina. Sometimes Dakshina was given in the form of villages. The Satvahana rulers also encouraged Buddhism by granting lands to the monks. Nagarjunakonda and Amaravati in Andhara Pradesh became important seats of Buddhist culture under the Satvahanas similarly Buddhism flourished in the Junar and Nashik areas in the Maharashtra where it appears to have been supported by the traders.

1.2.2 Polity and Administration

Polity and Administration under the Shung :

Though we have very little information of polity and administration during the Shung period on the basis of available information we can definitely say that it cannot be denied that it were the sungas who guarded the country from the onslaught of the Yavanas. If the Sungas had not established a strong government in the country and driven away the Yavanas the Yavanas might have succeeded in establishing their dominance over the entire Northern India and in that event the country would have been completely Hellenize.

Polity And Administration Under the Satvahanas :

Satvahanas have a prominent place in their history. They ruled according to Dharmashastras. The king was the upholder of Dharma and was represented as possessing the qualities of ancient gods like

Rama, Bhima, Keshava and Arjuna etc. This was obviously meant to ascribe divinity to the satvahana king. The Satvahanas kept some of the administrative units found in Ashokan times. Their district was called Ahara as it was known in the time of Ashoka and their officials were known as amatyas and Mahamatras as they were known in Maurya times. However their administrative parts were also called Rashtra and their high officials were known as Maharashtrikas. The Senapati was appointed provincial governor. The administration in the rural areas was placed in the hands of gaulmika who was a head of the military regiment consisting of, nine elephants, 25 horses and 45 foot soldiers. The head of the army platoon was therefore posted in the countryside to maintain peace and order. The military character of the satvahana rule is also evident from the common use of such terms as kataka and Skandhavaras in their inscriptions. These were military camps and settlements which served as administrative centres when the king was there. The Satvahanas started the practice of granting tax-free villages to Brahmanas and Buddhist monks. The cultivated fields and villages granted to them were declared free from molestation by royal policemen and soldiers and all other royal officials. These areas therefore became small independent islands within the Satvahana kingdom. The Satvahana kingdom had three grades of feudatories. The highest grade was formed by the king who was called Raja and who had the right to strike coins. The second grade was formed by the Mahabhaoja and the third grade by the Senapati.

1.2.3 Society

Social conditions during the Shunga and Satvahanas :

During this period also Varna and Ashrama system continued to rule the society. Society comprised of four various i.e. Brahman, Kshatriya, Vaishya and Sudra. The duties, status and occupations of these Varnas are enumerated in the Dharmasastras. The most important development in the Varna system is the increase in the number of mixed jatis. Just as society comprised of four varnas so too the life of an individual was divided into four stages that is Brahmacharya ashrama, Grihastha ashrama, Vanaprasth ashrama and Sanyasa shrama. The joint family system characterised the society.

Marriage between the members of the same jatis was preferred. The women enjoyed an honourable place in the society. Women were allowed some personal property (Stree-Dhana) in the form of jewellery, clothing etc.

Women not only got good education but also held honourable place in the household and society. Two classes of women students are mentioned-Brahmavadin or life long students of sacred texts and Sadyodvaha who pursued their studies till their marriage. They also received training in the fine arts like music, dancing and painting. We find the reference to the practice of sati also. Though the marriage between the members of the same jatis was preferred there are reference of anuloma and partiloma marriage anuloma marriage means male of higher Verna and female of lower varna and partiloma marriage means male of lower varna and female of higher varna. The social status of a person born of anuloma was higher than partiloma and they allowed their father's is occupation.

1.2.4 Economy

Economic conditions during the Shunga and Satvahanas

The period witnessed all round development in the field of agriculture, industry and trade. Agriculture was the chief occupation of a large number of people. Among the crops wheat, pulses, rice of different kinds, sesame, linseed, coarse grains, saffron, sugarcane, mustard and a large number of vegetables and fruits were grown. Noticeable advancement in trade and industry is made during this period. The literature of the period refers to eighteen types of guilds. The guilds defined rules of work and controlled the quality of the finished product and its prices to safeguard both the artisans and the customers. The guilds also acted as a banker, financer and a trustee. Trade is the main channel of distribution of industrial product. The items of trade were Indian spices, sea-products, sandal wood, pearls, metals, textiles of various types, semi-precious stones and animals.

Arikamedu was an important Roman settlement and trading station it was located close to a port. The number of hoards of Roman coins found in the Deccan and South India proves the volume of this trade in favour of India. Trade and contacts with Rome and the West was not the only commercial outlet open for India. India saw a increase in Indo-China relations and the introduction of Indian culture South East Asia. It has been mention as Suvarnabhumi in the literature of the period.

1.2.5 Culture

Culture under the Shung :

Sanchi, Bharhut and stupas are the best examples of Buddhist art and architecture that flourished during this period. The stupa is a hemispherical dome or mound built over sacred relics either of the Buddha himself or of a sanctified monk or a sacred text. The relics were generally kept in a casket in a smaller chamber in the centre of the base of the Stupa. The Stupa has a fenced path called Pradakshinapatha. At the four cardinal points there was a break in the railing because of gate ways. One of these gate ways was donate by the Guild of ivory workers of Vidisa. Most notable feature of this age was the evolution and propagation of Bhagwata Dharma. Patanjali a renowned scholar and the writer of the most outstanding work in the field of grammar 'Mahabhasya' which is commentary on a 'Asthadhyayi' is contemporary of pushymitra shung.

Culture under the Satavahana : In the Satvahana phase the two common religious Constructions were the Buddhist temple which was called Chaitya and the monastery which was called Vihara. The Chaitya was a large hall with a number of columns and the Vihara consisted of a central hall entered by a doorway from a verandah in front. The famous Chaitaya is that of Karle. It is about 40 meters long, 15 meters wide and 15 meters high. The Chaitaya of Karle consist of a fairly complicated structure all cut into the rock. The ceilings of a few of these chaitaya displays an imitatin of a barrel vault with wooden ribs. This point the impact of wooden construction in stone. The Vihara was excavated near the Chaityas for the residence of the monks during the rainy season. During the Satvahana period, Andhra Pradesh is famous for independent Buddhist structures mostly in the form of stupas. The most famous of them are Amaravati and Nagarjunakonda. The official language of the Satvahanas was prakrit. All inscriptions were composed in this language and written in the Brahmi script.

✧ EXERCISES ✧

Q. I : Answers of the following questions in 100 words.

1. Give the information of Indo-Greek king Menander ?
2. Explain the career and achievements of Saka king Rudradaman ?
3. What are the achievements of the Parthians ?
4. Explain the role of Kadphises I in the Kushanas dynasty ?
5. Give the information of the successors of Pushyamitra ?
6. Explain the polity and administration under the shung ?

Q. II : Write the Answers of the following questions in 300 words.

1. Explain the role of Pushyamitra Sunga in the Sunga dynasty ?
2. Give an account of the achievements of Gautamiputra Satakarni ?
3. Explain the social conditions during the period of the shung and Satvahanas ?
4. What is the cultural progress during the period of the Satvahanas ?

Q III : Write the answers of the following questions in 500 words.

1. Write in detail about the character and achievements of Kanishka ?
2. What is the Economic condition during the post-Mauryan period ?
3. Give the information of polity and administration under the Satvahanas ?

Q. IV : Write a short note on the following questions.

1. Kadphises II
2. Gandhara School of Art
3. Mathura school of Art
4. Sri Yajna Satakarni
5. Cultural progress under the shung

✿ ✿ ✿

UNIT – 2

EARLY HISTORY OF SOUTH INDIA

SYNOPSIS

INTRODUCTION

The earliest mention that we find about the people and kingdoms of South India are preserved in three forms - Ashokan inscriptions, Sangam literature and Megasthenese's accounts.

2.1 Period of Sangam Literature

Sangam age is the period from the first century A. D. to fourth century A. D. in the south when the literary works of various literatures were approved by the societies or the academics. Tamil is the language of the literature. It may be mentioned that Tamil is the oldest among the spoken and literary languages of south India and the earliest literature of this language is known as Sangam literature. From Ashokan inscriptions, Megasthenese's accounts, and Sangam literature it is clear that there have been a lot of cultural interactions between southern and northern India. The Sangam literature believes that the dynasties of Cheras, Cholas and Pandyas belong to immemorial antiquity.

2.1.1 Society and culture

Sangam literature scholars flourished in the Pandya kingdom where three Sangams (College of Tamil poets were held). Of those, the literature of two are lost. The third Sangam comprises only epics and anthologies. These are from the Tamil classics. From the first Sangam nothing has been saved. From the second Sangam, just a single work Tolkappiyam has come down to us. It is a grammatical treatise written in pattern of sutras, though it also throws tremendous light on the culture, beliefs, customs, manners and thoughts of the people.

The other Tamil classics of the age known to us belong to the Third Sangam. These are epics and anthologies and are grouped in schematic Anthologies : (1) Narrinai, (2) Kuruntogai, (3) Aingurunuru, (4) Padirrupattu, (5) Paripadal, (6) Kalittogai, (7) Agananuru, (8) Purananura, (9) Pattuppattu.

The whole collection includes 2,279 poems of various lengths from three to eight hundred by 473 poets. There are notes giving the name of its author, the occassion of the composition and other details at the end of the each poem. Only a portion of the vast literature has survived. Many inscriptions referring to Cholas, Pandyas and Cheras mention about the Sangam literature. The three kingdoms offered patronage to poets and other authors from time to time. The Sangam literature reflects the maturity of the Tamil language and started serving as a powerful elegant medium of literary expression about the society and culture. Sangam literature presents a true picture. The literary pieces bring forward the composite character and a result of blend of the two cultures - Dravidian and Aryan. It can be understood this way that the stories of Ramayana and Mahabharata were very well known to the people of the south - mention of God Shiva, struggle between Krishna and Asuras, presence of great fire under the ocean and Uttarakuru - the northern country. The Sangam literature also mentions about the translation of Mahabharata in Tamil by Perundevanar which is known as Bharatam. During the Sangam age, the king patronised poets and supported the development of various arts like music and dance. Various kinds of musical instruments were described like the drums and the flutes. The courts of the kings were enlivened by the bands of the musicians followed by the women who danced to the accompaniment of the music mixed dances in which men and women danced together are also mentioned. The poems mention to the popular beliefs and customs. The people believed in omens and astrology. There were fortune tellers, the rites were practiced which were supported to avert the mischief of demons. The banyan tree was considered the abode of gods. The eclipses were the result of snakes eating up the sun and moon. Crows were believed to announce the arrival of the guests.

The Vedic religion had made its place in South India is clear from the references to costly sacrifices made by the monarchs. The religious duties were held high in the society. Hindusim was the prominent sect of the age and the worship of Subramanya (Murugam) was very prominent. The other members of the pantheon are Shiva, Vishnu, Krishna, Balarama, Anantashayi and Ardhanarishvara. The impact of northern ideas over religion and philosophy are marked. Dance and music were interconnected with religion since early times.

The status of women in Sangam society was not equal to that of men either in theory or in practice. There were married women who had settled down as dutiful housewives. It is these women who either committed Sati or led a very hard life as widows after the death of their husbands. There were female ascetics of Buddhist or Jain Sangam like Kaundi Adigal and Manimekalai. There were also a large number of courtesans. Though women acted as bodyguards they were not recruited as soldiers, ministers or other advisers of the king. Women did not own property.

2.1.2 Early polities

The three powerful kingdoms of the Sangam age were Cholas, Pandyas and Cheras.

Cholas : The Cholas occupied the delta of the Kaveri river and the adjoining region. The region of Kanchi was also part of the Chola kingdom. It was situated towards the north-east of the Pandya kingdom. Earlier the Chola capital was Uraiyur, but later it was shifted to Puhar which came to be known as Kaveripattanam. It looks like that a Chola king known as Elara conquered Sri Lanka and ruled over it for about 50 years.

Karikala was the most distinguished of the early Chola kings. His two major accomplishments look to be the crushing defeat he imposed upon the joint forces of the Chera and Pandya kings and successful invasion of Sri Lanka. It seems that Karikala was defeated in a great battle at Venni a confederacy of about a dozen rulers headed by Chera and Pandya kings. This effected his mastery over all of the Tamil country. Karikala maintained a strong navy and conquered Sri Lanka. He is credited to have built a large irrigation channels by means of building a 160 km long embankment along the river Kaveri. He fortified the famous sea port of Puhar. All this lead to the growth of agriculture, trade and commerce. He was a great patron of education and literature. He was a follower of the Vedic religion and performed many vedic sacrifices. After Karikala, the Chola empire declined and the Cheras and Pandyas extended their domination at the cost of the Chola land.

Pandyas : The Pandyas had an ancient past. The Pandya kingdom occupied roughly the part of the modern districts of Madurai, Ramnad and Tirunelveli in Tamil Nadu. The capital of the Pandya kingdom was Madurai. The Sangam literature gives some scattered information and names of a few kings. Nedunjeliyan is referred as a great Pandya king.

The Chola, Chera and five other small provinces combined against him at Madurai. But he defeated the joint forces. This great victory was remembered for a long period. He may be taken to have ruled around A. D. 210. He is also said to have performed many Vedic sacrifices. Under the Pandyas, the capital Madurai and port city Korkai were great centers of trade and commerce. The traders profited from trade with the Roman empire. The Pandyan kingdom was very wealthy and prosperous. Pandya kings sent embassies to the Trojan and the Roman emperor Augustus.

Cheras : The Cheras also known as Keralaputras were situated to the west and north of the Pandya kingdom. The area of the kingdom included the narrow strip of land between the sea and the mountains of the Kokan range. Like the Cholas and the Pandyas, the Chera rulers also take a high place in the history of South India. Nedunjeral Adan, the Chera king suppressed the Kadambas with their capital at Vanavasi (Near Goa). With the father of Chola king Karikala he fought a battle in which both the kings were killed. He is said to have defeated the Greeks and Romans who came in big numbers as traders and set of large colonies in South India. The greatest king of Chera dynasty was Senguttuvan according to the Chera tradition. He is said to have subjugated the Pandya and the Chola kings. But the important truth about these three early kingdoms of South India is that they regularly fought with each other and also with Sri Lanka.

Sangam Polity :

During the Sangam age, Tamils were ruled by vigorous kings. There were three crowned monarchs in Tamilaham. They were called as Vendar. The most common form of government in the Sangam age was hereditary monarchy. The eldest son of the reigning king mostly succeeded his father and the throne was inherited by him as a matter of right. The system of succession was the same in Chera, Chola and Pandya kingdoms and it was Patrilineal. There is no evidence to show that a woman ever succeeded to the throne in her own right. When a king ascended the throne there was a coronation ceremony.

Position of the king :

The crowned kings of the Sangam age held an impressive court. The royal court was called Arasavai or Vettavai. This court was the centre of the political activities of the king. It was an open court to which the members of the royal family, the officers of the crown and members of the public had access. The king was surrounded by the chief Government officials and generally some poets or other favourites. The king had certain basic functions and those were learning, performing sacrifices making presents, protecting the subjects and punishing the wicked and the guilty. There is no evidence that any king was deposed during the Sangam period but many kings voluntarily abdicated on certain occasions. The royal emblem of the Chola kings was the tiger that of the Cheras the bow and that of the Pandyas the carp. The umbrella circular in shape large in size and spotless white in colour was a visible emblem of royalty among the Tamil sangam rulers. The royal umbrella accompanied the king in the battlefield. Each Sangam king was an autocrat whose powers could not be checked or curtailed by institutional devices. It was the duty of a king to protect his subjects from all kinds of dangers, big and small, to look after the welfare of the people and maintaining law and order. The king must have strong army of which the others were afraid. The Sangam kings were aware of their responsibilities. The kings had their advisers whom they consulted if they wished and accepted their advice if they felt like doing so though the advisory bodies existed their advice could be rejected. The king was an absolute sovereign. The king was the chief executive and the highest judge whatever laws were made, were made by the king. There was no human power to punish him if he broke those laws. Divine qualities were assigned to the king. The king was identified with god. The divine right of the king to rule was fully accepted.

Two institutions : Two institutions called Aimperukulu and Enperaym are mentioned in many Tamil Sangam texts. The absence of a detailed description of these institutions in the Sangam texts has led to different interpretaions.

Ministers : The king employed many ministers and they were present in the court and advised the king on matters on which they were consulted. It was the duty of a minister to try to guide the king. There was no definite commitment that the ministers must be selected from any particular community.

Ambassadors : The kings of the Sangam age employed ambassadors they were the representatives of one king in the court of another.

Spies : Spies were employed by the king in large numbers. They were called orrar. Espionage was a permanent institution in the

Sangam polity and was not suspended during peace time but only became more intense in war - time. They had to spy on local persons as well as on foreigners. This was an burdensome task and involved considerable risk.

Municipal and village Government : The people of a village governed themselves through rich, influential, experienced and wise men of the villages. A small villages assembly called Avai met in the village to handle local problems. The village institutions of manram and podiyil were concerned mainly with the arbitration or petty disputes arising in the village. In the town arrangements were made for the supply of essential municipal services.

Warfare : During the Sangam age the art of warfare was fairly advanced. King was an inherent part of the army. He led his army in person and was at the head of his army. He displays a tremendous bravery on the battlefield. The Tamil armies were well-equipped with the necessary arms of war. There was a very large variety of offensive and defensive weapons. Among the weapons of destruction were the lance or the spear, the bow and the arrow and the swords.

Law and Justice : The king give out justice with the help of such men as he thought suit for the job. There were law courts both in urban and rural areas. The king in the capital town and his agents at other places presided over those courts. The court in the capital town was called Avai and the court in the village was called Manram. Complaints were heard and enquired into and cases were decided. A trial in a royal court was a simple affair while in the village court it was simpler. The parties and witnesses were called upon to depose on oath. The king was the supreme judge. At times he acted as a policeman and a detective also. In the Sangam age punishments for theft was beheading Adultery was considered a serious crime punishment for adultery was capital punishment prostitution of a professional nature was not considered objectionable. The non-payment of land revenue was considered a civil offence and punished accordingly. The punishments awarded for crimes in the Sangam age included decapitation mutilation of the offending limbs of the body, torture and imprisonment and imposition of fines payable mostly in kind. Confession in the court was followed by prescribed punishment duly awarded by court.

2.2 Economy

The Sangam literature poems speak of trade and commerce as well. This information is supported by the archaeological finds. Although the Chola, Pandya and Chera states were weakened by the wars, they greatly profited from their natural recourses and foreign trade. The Sangam economy was simple and mostly self-sufficient. The people were industrious.

2.2.1 Towns, Trade and Crafts

Agriculture, fishing and hunting were the major businesses. A large number of persons were engaged in industries and commerce both inland and foreign. The major towns like Puhar, Kanchi, Vanji, Uraiyur, Tondi, Madurai, Musiri etc. absorbed most of these manufactured goods. Industry was encouraged on account of a rising demand in foreign markets. Shipping and other allied industries like harbour-building and warehouse construction were developed to sustain foreign trade. The chief occupation of the people was agriculture. The main product was paddy. Indigenous industries were fairly advanced like spinning and weaving were the most important and widely practised crafts. Weaving was a specialised industry in certain very important towns like Madurai, Uraiyur etc. The textile products were known for their beauty and fitness. The smithy was an another important industrial factory where weapons of war were forged and repaired. Carpentry was a very common industry. There was both internal and foreign trade at that time. Generally, industry and trade were carried on by groups of hereditary craftsmen. Barter system played an important part in all transactions. There were well established markets or bazars called Angadi in the bigger towns.

These markets had huge buildings. Integrity in trade was generally appreciated. There were two types of traders one who manufactured and sold goods at the place of manufacture and those who went about selling the goods. There was an extensive trade with foreign countries. Pepper, ginger, rice, cardamom, cinnamon, turmeric sandal-wood, ayil, almug, gems, corundun, cotton and cotton facbrics, ivory, pearls were certain commodities which were in great demand in foreign markets. There was trade with Rome and Greece. A large number of Roman gold coins of the Augustan age have been found in many parts of South India. There were direct trade routes between South Indian states and with Rome, Egypt and Arabia. Ship-building was a local industry in south India. Goods were collected in warehouses which were built on the beach and were located in the ships going abroad.

Revenue and Finance :

In the Sangam age many varieties of taxes were known and collected out of that revenue the king adjusted his private and public spending. A number of officials were enrolled by the king to look after the revenue matters. The most important source of revenue was the land tax. It was called Irai or Karai. Tolls and customs duties were called Ulgu or Sungam. The rate of land revenue was 1/6 of the produce of the land on particular occasion the payment of land revenue was remitted. It was competent for the king to assign a tax-free lands of certain person or institutions. Next to the land revenue were the customs duties and tolls Tamilaham had and extensive trade with places like Java, Rome, Burma, Egypt and Malaya. The goods imported and exported were of such form and in such quantities that even a nominal toll would have brought alot of revenue to the king. Some income must have come by the way of fines paid by criminals who were found guilty. The tax collectors were given the direction that they should collect the tax in such a way that the assesses do not feel the burden of tax.

✧ EXERCISES ✧

Q. I : Write the answers of the following questions in 100 words.

1. Explain the period of Sangam Literature ?
2. Position of women during the period of Sangam Literature ?

Q. II : Write the answers of the following questions in 300 words.

1. Explain the contribution of the Cholas during the period of Sangam Literature ?
2. Evaluate the role of the Pandyas during the age of Sangam society ?
3. What is the achievement of the Cheras during the Sangam age ?

Q. 3 : Write the answers of the following questions in 500 words.

1. Discuss the condition of society and culture during the Sangam period ?
2. What is the economic condition during the Sangam age ?

Q. 4 : Write a short note on following.

1. Chola king Karikala
2. Pandya king Nedunjeliyan

✿ ✿ ✿

UNIT – 3

NORTH INDIA : GUPTA AND HARSHAVARDHAN

SYNOPSIS

INTRODUCTION

The empire of the Kushanas and Satvahanas came to an end in the middle of the third century A. D. and a new dynasty was established in north India known as the Guptas. The Gupta kings were known not only for their political strength in the Indian history, but also for great success in the field of administration, society, trade and science and technology etc.

3.1 The Gupta Empire

About the early Guptas we do not know much in detail. According to the Allahabad pillar inscription of Samudragupta, Srigupta and Ghatotkachagupta are his ancestors. The Puranas mention that the early Guptas controlled the area along the Ganga, Prayag, Saketa and Magadha.

3.1.1 Brief political History

Chandragupta I : It is accepted popularly that Chandragupta I (son of Ghatotkacha and grandson of Srigupta) was the real founder of the great Gupta empire. He was a great warrior and a statesman. He was responsible for establishing a stable and strong government. In this great task his marriage with a Lichchavi princess Kumaradevi proved very useful as is proved by the coins of Chandragupta I and Kumaradevi type. These coins portray the figures of Chandragupta and Kumaradevi and mention the name of the Lichchhavis. The Gupta Lichchhavis alliance was responsible for the function of the Gupta empire. Chandragupta I introduced a new era - the Gupta era starting with his coronation A. D. 320. He was the first Gupta king to adopt the title Maharajadhiraja and issued gold coins.

Samudragupta : Samudragupta succeeded his father Chandragupta I in about A. D. 340. He was the greatest military power leader of his time. He was chosen by his father as his successor because of his qualities that would make him into a good king. The most reliable source of information about Samudragupta is the Allahabad pillar inscription which gives a detailed account of the career and personality of Samudragupta. The inscription was composed by one of his officials, Harishena and engraved on the Ashoka's pillar at Allahabad. The military achievements of Samudragupra contain a long list of kings and rulers defeated and subduced by him. The Allahabad prashasti mentions that he conducted three military campaigns to complete the task. The first campaign was the North Indian campaign. In the Aryavarta, he uprooted nine kings and princesses and annexed their kingdom. His next most important campaign was in Southern India. In the inscription altogether twelve kings and princesses of the south (Dakshinapatha) are listed. In the case of the kings of this region he followed the policy of first capturing the kings, then releasing them from imprisonment and then reinstalling them as kings in their dominion. By showing royal mercy he won their loyalty. After these conquests he performed Ashvamedha yajna. On this occasion, he issued gold coins portraying the sacrificial horse and bearing the legend conveying that he performed the Ashvamedha sacrifice. The third campaign mentioned in the Allahabad pillar inscription was the list of fourteen kingdoms bordering his kingdom. These rulers thought it wise to conclude peace by an act of homage thus they paid tribute to Samudragupta, followed his orders and showed their respect by attending his court. Some forest kings (Atavika - rajas) are also mentioned whom Samudragupta had made his Paricharaka (helpers).

Another group of political powers mentioned in the inscription are such as Sakas, Kushanas, Murundas as well as Simhalas (Sri Lanka) and inhabitants of other islands. These rulers sent embassies to Samudragupta's court. The king of Ceylon (Sri Lanka) Meghavarna requested Samudragupta for permission to build a monastery for the Buddhist pilgrims at Bodh Gaya. Samudragupta was not only an expert in war, but also in the Sastras. He is called Kaviraja i.e. 'King of poets'. He was a great poet, musician and a patron of learning. This is also supported by his lyricist type of coins which show him playing the Veena. He was liberal in his patronage of art and culture. Vasubandhu, the great Buddhist scholar flourished at his court. He died in about A. D. 380 and was succeeded by his son Chandragupta II.

Chandragupta II : The Gupta empire reached its highest glory both in terms of territorial expansion and cultural excellence under Chandragupta II. Like his father Chandragupta II was chosen by his father as his successor. Chandragupta II further extended the Gupta empire. He established matrimonial alliance with Vakatakas and married his daughter Prabhavatigupta to Rudrasena II of the Vakataka dynasty. Chandragupta II possibly concluded this alliance with the Vakatakas before attacking the Sakas so as to be certain of having a friendly power to back him up in Deccan. After the death of Rudrasena II, Prabhavatigupta acted as a regent on behalf of her two minor sons. Chandragupta II greatest achievement was his victory over the powerful Sakas dynasty. The annexation of their flourishing kingdom consisting of Gujarat and part of Malwa not only strengthened the Gupta empire, but also brought it into direct contact with western sea sports. This gave an enormous impetus to overseas trade and commerce. Ujjain became the second capital of the Gupta empire after the conquest. It is possible that after this victory over the Sakas that Chandragupta II adopted the title of Vikramaditya. Chandragupta II issued silver coins to mark his victory over Saka kshatrapas.

The exploits of a king called Chandra are glorified in an iron pillar inscription fixed near Qutub Minar in Delhi. This king Chandra of iron pillar is generally identified as Chandragupta II. Than it would appear that he established Gupta authority in north-western India and in a substantial part of Bengal.

Other than his conquests Chandragupta II's reign is remembered for his patronage of literature and arts. Kalidas, the great Sanskrit poet was a member of his court. During Chandragupta's reign the Chinese pilgrim Fa-Hien visited India and wrote an elaborate account of the life of its people.

Kumargupta I : Chandragupta II was succeeded by his son Kumargupta I. The epigraphic records show that he organised the administration of a vast empire and maintained its peace, prosperity and security for a long period of forty years. This is no small achievement upon his ability and tact. Like his grandfather Samudragupta he issued Ashavamedha type of coins. At the end of Kumaragupta's rule the Gupta empire was challenged by the Pushtamitras a community living on the banks of Narmada. SkandaGupta son of Kumaragupta I and future ruler fought and subdued them and restored peace.

Skandagupta : Kumargupta I was succeeded by his son Skandagupta. He was successful in establishing the prestige of Guptas which had suffered due to the constant attacks of the Huns. Peace and order was restored. The continuous foreign attacks and wars weakened the Gupta dynasty and after the death of Skandagupta, the empire seems to have suffered from wars of succession. The weak successors of Skandagupta were unable to repel the invasion of Huns who about the middle of the sixth century had forced an entry into Northern India and their king Toramana was reigning in Malwa.

Causes for the downfall of the Gupta Empire :

For nearly 250 years the Gupta empire provided political unity, good administration and economic and cultural progress to North India. The period therefore has been rightly regarded as the most glorious epoch in Indian history. But then it disappeared from the scene.

The difficulties of the empire began during the alter peiod of the reign of Kumar Gupta I. SkandaGupta faced them successfully but could not finish them. The difficulties were converted into weaknesses after him when his weak successors failed to rise to the occasion. This led to the disruption and finally to the extinction of the empire. The Gupta empire also met the fate of the Maurya empire and the causes too more or less were similar Skanda Gupta successfully checked the invasion of the Hunas as a crown prince and as an emperor he inflicted a crushing defeat on them. He also succedded in eliminating completely. The threat posed by pushyamitras to the empire. Yet these campaigns heavily taxed the financial and military resources of the empire. There for he was forced lo lower the quality of his gold coins. It meant that the empire was under financial strain.

However Skanda Gupta was successful.

But after him the Gupta rulers proved incompetent. Their incompetence increased the number of internal and external enemies. The provincial governors began to assert independences right from the reign of Puru Gupta. Emperor Budhagupta was hardly able to maintain a show of suzerainty over his governors.

After him even the nominal suzerainty was thrown off by the governors and they became independent ruler. The same way the later Gupta rulers failed to face their external enemies like the Vakatakas and the Hunas. Thus the incompetence of the Gupta rulers after Skanda Gupta was one of the primary causes of the downfall of the empire. In the absence of competent rulers no empire could be preserved in those times. The Guptas also lost their empire primarily because of their own incompetence.

Another factor which brought rain to the Gupta rulers was their own internal dissensions. After Kumaragupta the succession to the throne was always disputed probably even Skanda Gupta had to fight against Puru Gupta to get the throne. And after the death of Puru Gupta the rival princes of the family fought against themselves and the empire was divided.

Probably for a few years Narsimha Gupta ruled in Magadha while at the same time Vainya Gupta ruled over the eastern part of the empire and Budha Gupta who ascended the throne in 477 A.D. was not the ruler of a consolidated empire, but rather the head of a federal state.

After him even the Semblance of unity was overthrown and different Gupta princes or rulers took opposite side in the struggles and political conclusions of their period. This certainly helped in bringing about the downfall of the empire.

Put together the incompetence of the later Gupta rulers and their internal conflicts weakened the central authority which encouraged both external and internal enemies of the empire to take advantage of it. While the Vakataka rulers and the Hunas endangered the Imperial territories from outside the provincial governors broke up the unity of the empire from within by asserting their independence.

The success of Yasovarman in Malwa encouraged others. The Maitrakas assumed independence at valabhi, the Maukharis created an independent kingdom in the upper Gnges valley and the Gandas Wrested Bengal from the Guptas. The weak Gupta rulers failed to check the disintegration of the empire. When the Gupta empire weakened the Vakataka rulers (Who actually have matrimonial alliance with the Guptas during the time of Chandragupta II) tried to take advantage of it. Narendra sen attacked the territories of the empire in Malwa, Kosala and Mekhala during the period of Budha Gupta which weakend the authority of the Guptas in Madhya Pradesh and Bundelkhand. Afterwards the Vakataka ruler Hansen also attacked the boundaries of the empire. These attacks of the Vakataka rulers were primarily responsible for weakening the authority of the Guptas in Malwas, Gujarat and Bundelkhand and encouraging their governors to assett their independence.

A few scholars have expressed the view that the invasions of the Hunas were primarily responsible for the downfall of the Gupta empire. But it is not generally accepted. The view expressed by Dr. R.C. Majumdar is more tenable and now generally accepted. He says that the invasion of the Hunas were not primarily but only partially responsible for the downfall of the empire. The Hunas were defeated so severely be Skanda Gupta that they did not dare to invade the empire for about the next fifty years. And when they started their attacks again the empire had already become Weak because of its internal dissensions of course the Huna Kings Toramana and Mihirakula succeeded in penetrating deep into the Indian territories as far as the borders Magadha. But then at that time they were not fighting against the lively and might Gupta empire but against its ghost. The mighty Gupta empire was already dead. At that time it existed only in name. The Hunas did not contribute in any way to its death. Infact the kingdom of Toramana did not cross the river Indus and Mihirakula was defeated twice here once by Yasovarman of Mandasor and once by Narsimha II of Gupta dynasty. However it is accepted that their attacks no doubt put a heavy pressure on the financial and military resources of the empire and therefore were partially responsible for its downfall.

Dr. H.C. Raychaudhury puts forward a different reason for the downfall of the empire. He says that the later Gupta rules were influenced by Buddhism and its principle of non-violence. This brought about a negative influence on their military strength and that also contributed partially to their downfall. The later kings such as Rudra Gupta, Tathagata Gupta and Narsimha II was inclined towards Buddhism. It is stated that Narsimha II once captured Mihirakula but left him free on the advice of his Buddhist mother. Such acts connot be justified in matters concerning state politics and none would deny that the attitude of non-violence is harmful to the military strength of a state and thus creats danger to its existence. The later Gupta rulers definitely failed to maintain their military strength and thereby to purse a forceful policy against their external enemies and internal dissenters which certainly resulted in the downfall of the empire.

After Budha Gupta there existed virtually no Gupta empire as such. Narsimha Gupta was simply the ruler of Magadha. The rest of the empire was lost by him. Afterwards Magadha was also occupied by Maukhari ruler near about 544 A.D. ISanavarman. Thus ended the mighty Gupta empire. The internal weakness of the empire was primarily responsible for its downfall though of course external attacks also contributed to it.

3.1.2 Administration

The various inscriptions during the Gupta period throw light on their education, training, self-discipline and their devotion to the welfare of the subjects.

Monarch : Gupta rulers adopted epithets of Maharjadhiraja and Parambhattaraka as well as Param Daivata. The Allahabad pillar inscription described Samudragupta as a god who came down to live upon this earth. He was also described as equal to the Gods Kubera, Varuna, Indra and Yama. Efforts for material and moral uplift and progress of the subjects. Internal Security and protection from external danger were regarded as the responsibility of an ideal ruler. The eldest son was to succeed the king. On the post of provincial governors usually the king's younger brothers were appointed. The king enjoyed absolute authority. He was the centre of all military, political, administrative and judicial powers of the kingdom. The secretariat at the capital worked under his personal direction and supervision. The provincial governors and their subordinates were under his control and guidance. He was expected to carry out laws and rules that were framed not by himself but by the wise saints and Rishis of the beyond age. Wide authority was given to the local self governing institutions like the village panchayat and town councils.

Ministry : The king carried on the administration on with the help of a ministry. The crown prince and the feudatory chiefs also assisted in the administration. The smritis and inscriptions frequently mention to Ministers as Mantries or Sachiv. Military leadership was one of the important qualifications necessary for ministers of the state.

Central Government : The capital of the kingdom was the headquarters of the central government, i.e. the Central Secretariat. Its chief officer was called Sarvadhayaksha. He was a link between the central and provincial government. He used to convey the orders of the central government to the provincial and district officers. Some of the high imperial officers were Sandhivigrahika (Minister of peace and war, foreign affairs), Mahabalad-hikritas (Commander-in-chief), Mahadandanyaka (judge or prefect of police), Akshapataladhikrita (Lord keeper of state documents) Mahapratihara (In charge of the staff of Pratiharas), Sthapaid Samrat (Officer-in-charge of harem), Rajastaniya (officer-in-charge of the place), Pratyantpal and Antapal the governor and administrator frontier region. The officers of troops were paid salaries. There were a number of Mahasenapatis under the king and they had their armies that were posted in different provinces. Fighting force was divided into infantry, cavalry and the elephant troops. Taxes were paid partly in kind and partly in cash. The government made elaborate arrangements for the proper administration of granaries. Forests and mines of salt and metals were the state property and were properly administered by the revenue department. The administration of waste lands which were also a property of the state was left in the hands of the municipal board or the village council in whose jurisdiction they were situated. Hindu traditions required the king to administer justice himself when he was present at the capital. The judicial system was far more developed under the Guptas than in earlier times. Many law - books were compiled during this period and for the first time civil and criminal laws were clearly demarcated. Theft and adultery fell under criminal law, disputes regarding various types of property under civil law. Elaborate laws were laid down about inheritance. The guilds of artisans, merchants and others were governed by their own laws.

Two new classes of officers were introduced by the Guptas. These were Sandhivigrahika - the minister of peace and war i.e. modern foreign minister - he worked in close co-operation with the king and the military department. He was required to be a great diplomat and kumaramatyas a body of top ranking officials attached not only to the king but also to the crown prince and sometimes placed as in charge of districts. They were like modern civil servants. Another class of important officials were Ayuktas probably the same as Yuktas mentioned in the Ashokan inscriptions.

Provincial Administration : The provinces were further divided into Bhuktis and Vishyas. These provinces were not of the same size. The provinces were known as Desha. Viceroys of the provinces were appointed by the emperor. It was their duty to protect the provincial territories from external attack and to keep the internal peace and order. It was duty of the viceroys to undertake works of public welfare e.g. construct tanks and other works of irrigation, construct and repair the works of public utility and promoting peace and order. They were supposed to create confidence among the people.

The District Council and Administration : The different officials who assisted Vishyapati in the work of district administration were : Pustapala the officer in charge of records which showed right dimension of land both cultivated and non cultivated situated within the district. Saulkika-was the superintendent of tolls and customs. Gaulmika was the superintendent of forests and woods. Druvadhikarutka was the superintendent of the collection of the royal share in agricultural produce. Agraharka was the superintendent of charities and Karnika was the registrar. Administration of justice in important towns and cities was carried on by specially appointed officers. The seals of Dharmashasandhikarna, Nayadhikarna and Dharmadhikarna were the seals of courts of justice functioning at important provincial and district centres.

Village and town Administration : The jurisdiction of village authorities extended over houses, streets, bazars, wells, tanks, temples, cemeteries, waste lands, forests and cultivable lands. All lands cultivable and non cultivable were measured by officers known as Simakaras. Agriculture was the chief occupation of the people but each of them had usually their own compliment e.g. potters, oil-men, cobblers, black-smiths, weavers, carpenters. Gramadhyaksha was the head of the village administration. The town administration was carried on by an officer known as Purapala. He was helped by the town council known as parishad.

Judiciary and popular courts : There were judges at the headquarters of a district. In a village, justice was administered by royal officials with the help of the members of the village council. Popular Courts of the time were the Panchayatas in towns and villages.

Extent of the Empire : The Gupta empire comprised of Bengal, Bihar, the Uttar Pradesh, Eastern Punjab, portion of central provinces, central India including Malwa, North Gujarat, Kaithawar which included the thriving parts of cambay Ghogha, Veraval, Porbander and Dvaraka.

3.1.3 Society

The account of social life in India during the Gupta age is well described by Fa-Hien. In the time of the Guptas, Hindu society was divided into four castes viz. Brahamanas, Kahatriyas, Vaishyas and Sudras. There were four Ashram's through which every individual had to pass and those were Brahmacharya, Grihastha, Vanaprastha and Sanyas. Certain duties were prescribed for the various ashramas or stages of life. There was slavery in society, but it was mild in its incidence Fa-Hien noticed the general practice of non-violence. There was a tendency to lower the age of marrying girls. The rule was that the guardian should marry the girl before puberty. During the Gupta period joint family system continued to be a chief feature of Hindu private life. The ownership of the family property was vested in the father but the rights of the different sons and brothers to their separate shares were recognised. The laws about women under the Guptas clearly prove that their status in society had been considerably raised. For the first time in the history of Hindu law, the right of a woman to inherit was fully recognised in the Yajnavalkya Smriti. Widows led a simple and ascetic life and they received maintenance from the family. Both the men and women were fond of ornaments. Soldiers and officials received a regular salary and corruption was absent.

3.1.4 Trade

In the Guptas age, there was flourishing trade both internal and external. The main articles of internal trade were cloth, salt, spices, food grains, bullion and precious stones. This trade was carried on by road and through rivers. The main items of export from India were silk, pearl, spices of various kinds, textiles, ivory, sea produce, precious stones, cloths, indigo, perfumes, drugs, incense, cocoanut. Tamralipti, Sopara, Arikamedu, Barbaricum, Brighukachchha, Muziris, Kaveripattnam, pratishthana were the important sea ports of the time. These were well connected through inland routes from all parts of India. The main items of import were tin, gold, lead, silk, corals, copper, dates, copper, camphor and horses. During this period, India maintained regular maritime relation with Sri Lanka, Africa, Persia, Arabia, Byzantine Empire and further west. In the eastern part India developed commercial relations with China, Burma and South East Asia. Gupta rulers facilitated trade by building and maintaining lighthouses at the necessary points and by keeping sea routes free and safe from pirates. The various branches of industry were maintained at the same high level as in the earlier period because of abundance of raw materials and the skill and enterprise of the artisans and the craftsmen. Big ships were built. Guilds (shreni) were well organised during this period. Some of guilds also performed banking operations to provide capital for their members.

The highly flourishing trade and commerce made the country tremendously wealthy and the reputation of the richness of India spread far and wide. In the beginning of the fifth century the people of the 'Middle Kingdom' according to Fa-Hien were happy and prosperous. Description of the city, dwelling houses ornaments, wealth and luxurious items etc. in literary accounts prove the high standard of living and the luxury of town life.

Gupta Coinage :

Gupta coinage in the first place the Gupta coins are perfect art of coinage. Secondly they indicate India's is prosperity during the Gupta age. Thirdly they help us in establishing, the extent of the Gupta empire and the areas of Gupta influence. Fourthly they throw light on some important historical fact and lastly they level the personal accomplishments and achievements of the emperors.

Chandragupta I : Chandragupta I issued his coins with the figure of his queen Kumardevi the Lichchavi princess.

Samudragupta : Samudragupta issued gold coins of various types like tiger type. lyricist type, Asvamedha type, Standard type and the archer type of coins.

Chandragupta II : We have a large number of coins of Chandragupta II archertype, couch type, chhattra type, lion slayer type and horseman type of coins. On one of his coins Golddes Lakshmi with her lotus seat was carried on.

Kumargupta I : Kumargupta I issued archer type, Asvamedha type, horseman type, lion slayer type, tiger-slayer type and elephant - rider type etc. Most of the coins of Kumargupta I were like, the coins issued by his predecessors but the elephant rider type was introduced by Kumargupta I. He also issued another new coin with the figure of Kartikeya ridding his peacock.

3.1.5 Science and Technology

In the field of Science and Technology India had much advanced knowledge during this period in comparison to any other country in the world. In mathematics, Aryabhatta wrote the book Aryabhattiya. It is divided into four parts. As regards geometry. Aryabhatta considers among other topics, an area of a triangle, the theorem on similarity of triangles, the area of a circle and the theorem relating to rectangles contained by the segments. The most significant characteristic of Aryabhata's mathematical system is his unique system of notation. It is based on the decimal place-value system. Brahmagupta the other famous mathematician wrote Brahma Siddhanta his another famous work was Khandakhadya. He developed rules for operating with negative qualities and with zero. He began to utilize algebra to astronomical problems. Varahamihira who flourished in the court of Chandragupta II has preserved in his Panchasiddhantika the accounts of five astronomical works which were considered as authority in his own time. These five Siddhantas are known as Surya, Romaka, Paulisa, Paitamaha and Vasishtha. The Surya Siddhant is the most important and complete work on the astronomy of the period. In the field of astrology. Varahamihira in his encyclopaedic book Brihatsamhita preserved a considerable amount of ancient knowledge on the subject. This book is not only important on natural astrology but also for veritable compendium of ancient Indian learning in the field of science. As in mathematics so too in astronomy, Aryabhatta was an outstanding scholar of the Gupta age. His most original contribution was that the eclipses were not the work of Rahu but were caused by the shadow of the earth falling on the moon therefore asserting the movement of earth on its own axis around the sun as was known in Vedic times. He was the first to utilize sign functions in astronomy. He also discovered an accurate formula to measure the decrease or increase in the duration of two consecutive days. As regards Ayurveda, the great writer of this period is Vagabhata. The two famous books of the period are Astanga - sangraha and the Astanga - hridaya - Samhita assigned to two different authors by the same name i.e. Vagabhata. There were also treaties on the diseases of animals. The best known is Hastyayurveda while the other is Asvasastra.

The Mehrauli iron pillar is the best example of progress that is attained by the Indians 1500 years ago. This is 7.32 metres high with a diameter of 40 cm at the base to 30 cm at the top and a weight of about 6 tonnes. It has resisted all the vagaries of nature such as rains, cold and heat for over all these 1500 years without rusting.

Gupta Age the Golden period of Indian History :

(1) The Guptas were responsible for the unification of the country. They defeated the foreigners like Shakas and Kushanas.

(2) The Gupta's had a strong, efficient and well organised government. The government at the centre was very strong. The uniformity in the system of administration created a sense of unity among the people. Their military and civil services were very efficient. Their government aimed of the moral, material and intellectual welfare and general prosperity of the people.

(3) Guptas themselves were the followers of Brahmanism. They generously patronised Jainism and Buddhism.

(4) Guptas established their commercial relations with the western countries.

(5) The peace, order and stability as well as efficient government of the Gupta age gave a strong impetus to trade, commerce, craft and industry which resulted in the gain of wealth and subsequent general welfare of the people.

(6) Indian traders, merchants and missionaries along with poets, travellers went to distant land. They spread Indian civilization and culture in foreign countries like China, Java, Sumatra, Indo-China, Bali and Central Asia etc.

(7) Sanskrit language was patronised by the Gupta rulers. Many literary works of great merit were produced during this period. Kalidas the most brilliant luminary was patronized by Chandragupta II. Varahamihira was a great scholar, a man of encyclopedic learning and knowledge. His work Brihatsamhita is well-known treaties in astronomy. Arybhatta and Brahmagupta were the greatest mathematicians and scientists of this age. Chandragupta II's nine gems are famous. As mentioned earlier, Kalidasa adorned Vikramaditya's court. His dramas Malavikagnimitram, Abhijnanashakuntalam and Vikramorvasiyam are world famous, so also his poetical works Meghaduta, Raghuvamsa, and Kumarasambhava are of rare merit. Another famous dramatist was Dhara. Bhasa has been discovered that he wrote about fourteen plays famous among them are Urubjanga the Pratima Nutaka, the Pratinjnayu Gandhara and Svaphavasavadatta. Sudraka was another famous dramtist. He wrote the famous play Mrichchakatika - Little clay cart this play is considered one of the best plays of ancient India. Vishakhadatta famous plays are Mudrarakshasa and Devichandraguptam. Bharvi's epic poem. Kiratarjuniya dealing with an episode from the Mahabharat is known for its meaningful language. Bhatti in his Bhattikavya or Ravanavadha narrates the story of Rama. In

this work along with the story he very skillfully illustrates rules of grammar. Mention may also be made of three Shatakas of Bhartrihari. He has also been credited for writing the commentary on the Mahabhasya of Patanjali one of the most famous work of this period is Panchatantra written by Vishnu Sharma. The popular work Hitopadesa is based on the Panchatantra. This period is particularly memorable for the complication of the Amarakasha by Amarasimha, who was a scholar in the court of Chandragupta II. A few inscriptions of the period also possess in some degree most of the characteristic features of Sanskrit kavya. Harisena the author of Allahabad Prashasti, Vatsabhatti of Mandsor Prashasti, Vasula, Bandhuvirman and Kabja are some of the eminent composers of inscriptions.

(8) Some of the Gupta temples were built with bricks e.g. those in Uttar Pradesh, Madhya Pradesh, Bihar and Bengal. The world famous treasures of Ajanta are the best example of the art of painting during the Gupta period. The high standard of work shows a long tradition of art and a rich cultural background and of course, the royal patronage. The caves were selected for religious purposes and for the safety of the valuable work. The iron pillar at Delhi, the eight feet copper image of the Buddha shows their skill and knowledge of metallurgy. The seated Buddha at Sarnath and standing Buddha at Mathura are two other outstanding examples of sculpture. The Varaha at Udaygiri, Vishnu from Mathura and the Deogarh temple are examples of Hindu sculpture.

(9) Shiva and Vishnu were the popular deities along with mother goddess or Shakti. Yakshas and Nagas were worshipped. So also were the trees and the water. Buddhism was popular in Kashmir, Punjab and Afghanistan. Mathura, Saranath, Bodh Gaya, Nalanda, Kanchi, Ajanta and Praharpur were the places of the Buddhists.

(10)The growth of oversea trade induced many adventurous Indians to found colonies of their own in far - off lands particularly in East Indies. Then they carried with them their Indian religion and culture which flourished all the more in their new surrounding. Thus were sown the seeds which eventually sprouted forth into what is called the "Greater India".

3.2 Harshvardhan

The attacks of the Huns destroyed the Gupta empire and many small kingdoms were set up in the country which lasted about a century. One such kingdom was that of Pushyabhutis of Thaneswar. During this period there was no king powerful enough to suppress all these kingdoms. Finally, in the beginning of the 7th century Harshvardhan, the king of Thaneswar conquered almost the whole of Northern India and founded a powerful empire.

Sources of Information :

(1) Harshacharita (life of Harsha) was written by Banabhatta the court poet of Harsha. It is a biography of Harsha.

(2) Travels of Hiuen - Tsang : Hiuen Tsang the great Chinese pilgrim wrote an account of his travels which form a valuable source of information about the rule of Harsha.

Harshavardhan : He was one of the most noteworthy rulers of India. He ended political confusion in North India, built up a strong empire and provided it with an effective and efficient machinery. He belongs to the Pushyabhutis of Thaneswar. His father was Prabhakaravardhana. He set up friendly relations with Maukharis of Kanauj by marrying his daughter Rajyasri to king Grahavarman of Kanauj, Prabhakaravardhan died in 605 A.D. He was succeeded by his elder son Rajyavardhan. After some day, Rajayvardhan heard that Grahavarman was killed by the king of Malwa and ruler of Gauda Sasanka and Rajyasri was thrown into prison. Rajyavardhana marched to Malwa, but he was treacherously killed by Sasanka. Rajasri escaped. Harsh was crowned as the king in 606 A.D. Immediately, he decided to rescue his sister and punish Sasanka. He was successful in both the encounters.

His conquests : Kanauj was kingless after Grahavarman's death. The crown was offered to Harsha and he accepted it. He then started his conquests. He gathered a strong army. He won nearly the whole of North India. Bengal and Orissa (Now Odisha) came under him after Sasanka's death. The kings of Assam and Valabhi had recognized his supremacy. Harsha became the master of nearly the whole of North India. Harsha launched a campaign so as to extend his empire beyond the Narmada, but failed to do so. He was defeated at the hands of the Chalukya king Pulakesin II. Harsha's empire extended from the Punjab to northern Orissa and from the Himalayas to the banks of the Narmada.

3.2.1 Administration

Harsha kept a close watch over the entire system. He constantly toured in his kingdom to see that his officers were efficient. He was assisted by a council of ministers or Mantri Parishad. The kingdom was divided into Bhuktis or provinces, Vishyas or districts and Gramas or villages there was a revenue department to collect taxes.

It is true that theoretically the Government of Harsha was an autocracy but a large amount of self-government was allowed to the people in the irrespective areas. Most of the work was left in the hands of the village communities. Government of Harsha on the whole was a mixture of autocratic and democratic elements.

Council of Ministers : The king was assisted by a council of ministers. The council exerted itself whenever there was a vacancy to the throne. The council of ministers had a say not only in the choice of the king but also influenced foreign policy.

Secretariat : There seems to have been a well organised secretariat at the capital. The name of the chief officers of the state were Maharaja, Uparika, Sadhnika Mahasamanta, Paramatara, Vishayapati, Rajasthaniya etc. The superior civil service was manned by Kumaramatya. It is from them that ministers, Secretariat officers and district officers were taken. The centre had its own inspecting officers. It had also its own royal messengers. There is also a mention to an officer called Saravagatah who was probably a member of the secret service department. Most of the senior officers were paid in cash while the government servants of the lower grade were paid in cash or in land according to their work.

Military Administration : Hiuen Tsang tells us that it consisted of one lakh men. There were horses, elephants and camels also. Soldier normally enjoyed high prestige. Special care was taken to recruit soldiers. The horses were recruited from Sindh, Kamboja and Persia. Ordinary soldiers. Were called Bhatas and Chatas Cavalry officers were known as Brihadasvavara while Infantry officers were known as Baladhikritas. The commander - in - chief was known as Mahasenapati.

Judicial and Revenue Administration : Harsha' criminal laws were severe than those of Guptas. Cutting off the nose, ear, foot or hand was also found. Ordeals by fire, poison and water were common to determine the guilt of a person. Fines were imposed for minor crimes. Inspite of severe laws, crimes were common. Harsha received revenue from various sources. 1/6 of the produce was the land tax. There was sales tax, toll, tax and other minor taxes.

There is mention of three kinds of taxes viz. Bhaga, Bali and Hiranya. Bhaga was the land tax which was paid in kind. But it was difficult to ascertain which specific taxes were implied by the term Bali, while Hiranya refers to those taxes which were paid in cash by farmers and by merchants. Hiuen-Tsang tells us that taxation was very light. The crown lands were divided into four parts. The first part was for carrying out the affairs for the state. The second part was meant for paying the ministers and officers of the crown. The third part was meant for rewarding men of genius. The fourth part was meant for giving alms to religious communities.

3.2.2 Religion

Harsha's forefathers worshipped the Sun and Shiva. He was converted to Buddhism on the insistence of his sister and Hiuen - Tsang. He was influenced by the doctrine of Buddhism. Hiuen - Tsang mentions two most celebrated events of Harsha's reign, the assemblies at Kanauj and at Prayaga. The Kanauj assembly was held in honour of Hiuen - Tsang for whom the king had great affection and respect. Harsha and twenty other kings joined the huge procession from Bengal to Kanauj. Thousands of Buddhist monks,

Brahmans and Jains joined it. A large monastery was built at Kanauj and a high tower was also built. He donated large sums of coins and precious stones to religious scholars. He prohibited slaughter of animals. He built monasteries and stupas for Buddhist monks. He had secured a tooth, relic of Buddha from Kashmir. He sent missionaries for the spread of Buddhism.

After the ceremony at Kanuaj Harsha accompanied by Hiuen - Tsang proceeded to Prayaga where he used to celebrate religious festivals at the end of every five years at the meeting of the Ganga, the Yamuna and the Saraswati. Here, he performed the ceremony of 'Daan' which lasted for about three months. During these three months most of the collection of five years wealth was spent. According to a tradition, Harsha gave away everything except his personal clothing. Harsha attended six such assemblies at Prayaga in his lifetime and donated all he had.

3.2.3 Education

In the history of India, Harsha earned an undying reputation not so much for his conquests as for his peaceful activities. The great emperor was not only a patron of learning, but was himself and accomplished writer. He wrote three Sanskrit dramas - Priyadarsika, Ratnavali and Nagananda. He was a calligraphist too. He made arrangements for education and learning. He organized religious debates and conferences where people cleared their doubts about religion and philosophy. He had many learned men at his court of whom Bahabhatta the author of Harshacharita and Kadambari is the most well known. He was an ideal king and ranked among the noblest king of Indian History. Education was widespread during the reign of Harsha.

Nalanda University : Nalanda University was at the height of its fame. Several rajas and rich people had granted Jagirs and lands for its upkeep. The University of Nalanda had imposing buildings. There were at least 8 colleges built by different patrons including one by Balaputradeva king of Srivijaya. The colleges were built in rows. The Nalanda University had not only a magnificent building but all other kinds of facilities were also provided to students for their studies. The students were given free boarding and lodging. There were about 10,000 students and 1,500 professors of all kinds and they all lived like members of one family. The professors came from China, Korea, Japan, Tibet, Ceylon. Tukhara, Mongolia, Greater India and from different parts of India. Students were also came from different foreign Buddhist countries. There three great libraries called Ratnasagar, Ratnodadhi and Ratnaranjak. The Nalanda University was principally a Buddhist Vihara but in course of time subjects in addition to Buddhism also came to be taught. The subjects of study at Nalanda University were all the four vedas, grammar, medicine, logic, Yoga, Nyaya, Samkhya and the Buddhist works of the different schools. Sanskrit was the medium of instruction. Silabhadra a scholar of rare ability was the head of the university. The names of some of the most famous professors of the Nalanda University were Anga, Nagarjuna, Vasubandhu, Jinamitra, Archdeva, Dinnaga, Prabhamitra, Dharmapala, Chandrapala, Jnanachandra etc. The professors and students in Nalanda University were the followers and exponents of different sects or schools of thought. They were always meeting in debates and discussions. Nalanda University was a postgraduate institution to which admission was very hard. Before admission an examination was held in which hardly 20% students passed and the rest of 80% were rejected. Only the most brilliant were admitted to the University.

✧ EXERCISES ✧

Q. I : Write the answers of the following questions in 100 words.

1. Chandragupta I as the founder of the Gupta empire ?
2. The District council and Administration during the Gupta period ?
3. What is the administrative pattern during the period of Harshvardhan ?
4. How Harshvardhan was known for promoting education ?

Q. II : Write the answers of the following questions in 300 words.

1. Discuss the social conditions during the Gupta period ?
2. How did trade and commerce flourish during the Gupta period ?

Q. 3 : Write the answer of the following questions in 500 words.

1. Discuss the role of Samudragupta as an empire-builder during the Gupta age ?
2. Why is Chandragupta II known as the greatest of the Gupta emperors ?
3. Evaluate the administrative pattern during the Gupta age ?
4. How did science and technology develop during the Gupta period ?
5. Why is the Gupta age known as the golden period of Indian history ?
6. What are the achievements of Harshvardhan ?

Q. 4 : Write a short note of following.

1. Religious conditions during Harshvardhan's period ?
2. Nalanda University ?

✿ ✿ ✿

UNIT – 4

REGIONAL KINGDOMS : A BRIEF HISTORY

SYNOPSIS

INRODUCTION

The period after the death of Harsha in the mid seventh century A.D. and the establishment of Delhi sultanate in the twelfth century A.D. covers a span of 600 years. Since the days of Moukharis, Kanauj became the seat of power in North India a place which Pataliputra enjoyed before and Delhi was to enjoy afterwards. After the death of Harsha in A.D. 647 Kanauj lost its status as the capital city briefly. However in the beginning of the eighth century A.D. Kanauj came back as the centre of power with a very mighty king Yashovarman. He ruled over a vast empire which included almost the whole of northern India. He ruled till about A.D. 740. Kanauj from the sixth century A.D. till it finally fell to Mohammad Ghori in A.D. 1194 played an important part in the history of the North India and earned a position of not only a political centre but also a cultural centre.

4.1 The Chalukyas, Pallavas, Pandya – Struggle for Supremacy over Peninsular India

In Deccan and South India after the Satvahana rule had ended in the first half of the third century A. D. the Vakatakas rose to power in the second half of the third century A. D. The importance of the Vakatakas as a political power was recognized by Chandragupta II who married his daughter Prabhavati Gupta into the Vakataka family. After the Vakatakas three major kingdoms namely Chalukyas of Badami, Pallavas of Kanchipuram and the Pandyas of Madurai dominated the Deccan and South India for about 300 years.

4.1.1 The Chalukyas

As mentioned above the Vakataka power was followed by the Chalukyas of Badami, who played an important role in the history of the Deccan and South India for about two centuries until AD 757 when they were overthrown by their feudatories the Rashtrakutas. They ruled for about two centuries. The Chalukyas set up their kingdom towards the beginning of the sixth century in the Western Deccan. They established their capital of Badami or Vatapi in the district of Bijapur which today forms a part of Karnataka. We learn about the origin of the Chalukyas from Vikarmankdeva Charita of Bilhana. The Chalukyas claimed their descent from Brahma or Manu or the Moon. Perhaps the Chalukyas thought themselves as the sons of Gods. During this period no other power in the Deccan was as important as the Chalukyas of Badami until we come to Vijaynagar in later medieval period.

History of the Chalukyas : Jayasimha was the first Chalukya king. His son's name was Ranaraga. The Chalukya power had a modest start under both of them.

(1) Pulakesin I : Pulakesin I succeeded Ranaraga. He was the first great king among the Chalukyas. He ruled from about 535 to 566 A.D. He was the first independent ruler. He was the first Maharaja in his family in fact he is regarded as the real founder of the Chalukya dynasty. He took up titles such as Vallabha, Satyasraya, Rana-Vikrama etc. The inscriptions reveal that he had performed a number of Yajnas and sacrifices e.g. Hiranyagarbha, horse ceremony or Asvamedha, Agnishtoma and Vajapeya. He was a great scholar and had thoroughly studied the Puranas, the Ramayana, the

Mahabharata, Manava–Dharmasastra and other history. He is compared with such mythical heores as Yayati and Dilipa. According to a Badami inscription, he had laid the foundation of Vatapi fort. Though he is not credited with any specific conquest, however, he ruled over the present Bijapur district with his capital at Badami.

(2) Maharaja Kirtivarman I : Pulakesin I was succeeded on the throne by his son Maharaja Kirtivarman I from 567 A.D. to 598 A. D. He took up titles such as Vallabha, Satyasraya and Prithivi –Vallabha. He is also called as the first founder of Vatapi this shows that he beautified the town with temples and other buildings. It is stated in an inscription that Kritivarman defeated the rulers of Anga, Pandya, Magadha, Vanga, Cholas, Kalinga, Madraka, Ganga, Vattura, Mushaka, Kerala, Dramila, Aluka and Vaijyanti. Kirtivarman is also described as "Night of destruction" to the Nalas, Mauryas and Kadamabas. He is also stated to have broken up a confederacy of the Kadamba Kings. It appears that Kirtivarman annexed part of the Maurya territories in the Konkan.

(3) Mangalesa : In the year 598 A. D., Kirtivarman I died and was succeeded by his brother Mangalesa. The new king had ruled upto 610-611 A. D. He had assumed titiles such as Ranavikranta, Paramabhagavata etc. An Aihole inscription shows that he had secured victory over Kalachuris and Revati island. The Mahakuta inscriptions reveals that he had won a victory over Bodhraj or Budha a Kalachuri ruler and had confiscated his wealth and kingdom. Towards the close of his reign Manglaesa had to fight with his nephew Pulakesin II who was the son of Kirtirarman I. Mangalesa wanted his son to succeed him but Pulakesin II was against him. In the civil war, Mangalesa was killed and Pulakesin II became king.

(4) Pulakesin II : Pulakesin II was the greatest king of the Chalukya dynasty. He ruled from 610 - 11 A.D. to 642 A.D. He had the title of Sriprithivi - Vallabh, Vallabha, Parameshwara, Paramabhaga-vata and Prithivi-vallabh. The throne inherited by Pulakesin II was not a bed of roses he faced with two main problem :

(i) Protection of the country from foreign invasion.

(ii) On account of the civil war between Mangalesa and Pulakesin II the various parts of the Chalukya empire declared their independence to force these Jagirdards to accept his sovereignty. In such a situation Pulakesin II took a diplomatic and tactful step. He adopted the policy of divide and rule.

Conquests of Pulakesin II : After strengthening his power and resources Pulakesin II adopted a policy of aggression and aggrandizement. He brought under his authority all the neighbouring states. As regards the subjugation of his neighbours a detailed account is given in the Aihole inscription written by Ravikriti. In the south Pulakesin besieged and occupied Vanavasi. Vanavasi was the capital of Kadambas. Then he won over the Gangas of South Mysore and the Alupas friendship with the Kadambas was the chief reason of this victory. When the war was over the Ganga ruler married one of his daughters to Pulakesin II. In konkan he had won a victory over the Mauryas and occupied the city of Puri. Besides, he conquered the rulers of Latas, Malvas and Gurjaras. The country thus conquered brought Pulakesin II into contact with King Harsha of Kanauj. The Aihole inscription depicts his victory over Harsha of Kanauj. Hiuen-Tsang accounts reveal that the imperialistic ambition of two kings forced them to enter into a war. Both the kings wanted to occupy Gujarat. But Pulakesin II forced Harsha to be at a retreat. After defeating Harsha Pulakesin II assumed the title of Paramesvera. Now, no wonder Pulakesin II had became the head of three states namly Konkan, Karnataka and Maharashtra. He had also inflicted a crushing defeat on Mahendra Varman I the Pallava ruler. With the Cholas, Keralas and Pandyas he had established cordial relations. Thus, he had won manifold victories.

Death of Pulakesin II : It is true that the Pallavas had been defeated but they had not been completely crushed, Pulakesin II could not resist the Pallavas for long. Narsimhavarman the Pallava ruler and the son and successor of Mahendravarman I to wreck vengeance upon Pulakesin II invaded Badami and captured it Probably Pulakesin II was killed in this war.

Pulakesin II was not only the greatest Chalukya rulers, but also one of the greatest monarchs of ancient India. His fame and influence spread far and wide. A contemporary Muslim record shows that he had sent his ambassador in the court of the Persian king Khusro II.

(5) Vikramadiya I : Pulakesin II was succeeded by his youngest son Vikramdiya I. As Badami had fallen into the hands of the Pallavas his accession became difficult for sometime.

His Achievements : Vikramaditya attained his hereditary throne and crushed his enemies. He conquered the southern part of the Pallavas and restored the grants to gods and Brahmanas which had been confiscated by previous kings. He defeated Pallava king Narsimhavarman I, Mahendravarman II and Parmeshvaravarman I. In addition to this he occupied Kanchi too. He had established his authority on almost the whole of the Deccan.

(6) Vinayaditya : Vikramadita I was succeeded by his son Vinayaditya who ruled from A.D. 681 to 696. Contemporary records reveal that he had to wage a war against the ruler of Kanchi. He established his authority over the Pallavas, Pandyas, Keralas, Kalahras, Malavas, Aluvas, Vilas, Haihayas, Cholas and Gangas etc. He received an annual tribute from the rulers of Ceylon and of the valley of Kavera and Parasika. Towards the closing period of his reign he had to struggle hard against his enemies. His foes imprisoned his son Vijayaditya by this time Vinayaditya expired.

(7) Vijayaditya : Vinayaditya was succeeded by Vijayaditya who ruled from A. D. 696 to 733. His reign was a peaceful one. However, it appears that he was involved in a struggle with the Pallavas and the chief reason of it was his aggressive policy. He conquered Kanchi and levied tribute from Parameshvara-varman. Vijayaditya got constructed a beautiful Siva temple at Kanchi. He had a tolerant religious policy and he donated villages to Jain preachers. At Lakshmeshwar his sister got constructed a Jain temple.

(8) Vikramaditya II : Vijayaditya was succeeded by his son Vikramaditya II. He reigned from 734 to 745 A. D. one of his queens built the great temple of Siva at Pattadakal. Another queen built another great temple of Siva near the previous one. The Chalukyas had life long enemity with the Pallavas, Vikramaditya II in order to stamp out of Pallavas made surprise attacks upon them and received a heavy amount from Nandivarman. Then he entered the city of Kanchi. He did not destroy Kanchi but presented heaps of gold to the temple there. He also defeated the Pandya, Chola, Kerala, Kalabhra and other kings. He set up a pillar of victory on the shores of the Southern ocean. During his period, the Arabs made a fierce attack but they were given a shattering blow. Vikramaditya II was a great builder and patron of learning.

The End of the Chalukya Kingdom : Vikramaditya II was succeeded by his son Kirtivarman II who ruled from A.D. 746 to 757. He had helped his father in his Pallava campaign. He was the last king of the imperial line of Chalukyas. During his reign the Chalukya dynasty started hastening towards decay and downfall and within a short time the Rashtrakutas became all powerful in Southern India.

Chalukyas of Kalyani : The Chalukyas were able to revive their fortunes in 973 after over 200 years of dormancy when much of the Deccan was under the rule of the Rashtrakutas. The Western Chalukya kings belonged to the same family line as the illustrious Badami Chalukya dynasty of the 6th century while other Western Chalukya inscriptional evidence indicates show otherwise. Tailapa II, a Rashtrakuta feudatory ruling from Tardavadi – 1000 (Bijapur district) overthrew Karka II, re-established the Chalukya rule in the western Deccan and recovered most of the Chalukya empire. The Western Chalukyas ruled for over 200 years and were in constant conflict with the Cholas, and with their cousins, the Eastern Chalukyas of Vengi. Vikramaditya VI is widely considered the most notable ruler of the dynasty. He abolished the original Saka era and established the Vikrama Era. Under his leadership the Western Chalukyas were able to finish the Chola influence over Vengi (coastal Andhra) and become the dominant power in the Deccan. They went into their final dissolution towards the end of the 12th century with the rise of the Hoysala Empire, the Pandyas, the Kakatiya and the Seuna Yadavas of Devagiri.

Chalukyas of Vengi : Pulakeshin II captured the eastern Deccan, (coastal districts of modern Andhra Pradesh) in 616, defeating the remnants of the Vishnukundina kingdom and appointed his brother Vishnuvardhana as Viceroy in 621. After the death of Pulakeshin II, the Vengi Viceroyalty developed into an independent kingdom and consisted of the region between Nellore and Visakhapatnam. After the decline of the Badami Chalukya empire (mid-8th century), territorial disputes increased between the Rashtrakutas, and the eastern Chalukyas. For much of the next two centuries, the eastern Chalukyas had to accept subordination towards the Rashtrakutas. It was only during the rule of Bhima I (c.892–921) that these Chalukyas were able to manage some measure of independence. After the death of Bhima I, the Andhra region once again saw succession disputes and interference in Vengi affairs by the Rashtrakutas. Danarnava, the Chalukya king, was killed in battle in 973 by the

Telugu Chola King Bhima who then ruled over the region for twenty-seven years. During this time, Danarnava's two sons took refuge in the Chola kingdom. Chola Bhima's invasion of Tondaimandalam, a Chola territory, and his subsequent death on the battlefield opened up a new era in Chola–Chalukya relations. Saktivarman I, the elder son of Danarnava was crowned as the ruler of Vengi in 1000, though under the control of king Rajaraja Chola I. This new relationship between the Cholas and the coastal Andhra kingdom was unacceptable to the Western Chalukyas, who had by then replaced the Rashtrakutas as the main power in the western Deccan, but were unsuccessful. Telugu literature owes its growth to the eastern Chalukyas.

Histrorical Sources of Badami Chalukyas dynasty : Inscriptions in Sanskrit and Kannada are the main source of information about Badami Chalukya history. i.e. the Badami cave inscriptions of Mangalesha, Kappe Arabhatta record, Peddavaduguru inscription of Pulakeshin II, the Kanchi Kailasanatha Temple inscription and Pattadakal Virupaksha Temple inscription of Vikramaditya II provide more evidence. The Badami cliff inscription of Pulakeshin I, the Mahakuta Pillar inscription of Mangalesha and the Aihole inscription of Pulakeshin II (634) are examples of important Sanskrit inscriptions written in old Kannada script. The reign of the Chalukyas saw the arrival of Kannada as the predominant language of inscriptions along with Sanskrit. Several coins of the Badami Chalukyas with Kannada legends have been found. Travelogues by contemporary foreign travellers have provided useful information about the Chalukyan empire. The Chinese traveller Xuanzang had visited the court of Pulakeshin II. According to him Pulakeshin empire possibly covered present day Karnataka, Maharashtra and coastal Konkan. Persian emperor Khosrau II exchanged ambassadors with Pulakeshin II.

Society during Chalukyas : The Hindu caste system and 'devadasis' were recognised by the government. Kings had concubines (ganikas) who were given much respect, and Sati was perhaps absent. Sage Bharata's Natyashastra, the precursor to Bharatnatyam, the classical dance of South India, was popular and is seen in many sculptures and is mentioned in inscriptions. Some women from the royal family enjoyed political power in administration. Queen Vijayanka was a noted Sanskrit poet. Kumkumadevi, the younger sister of Vijayaditya (made several grants and had a Jain basadi called Anesajjebasadi constructed at Puligere, and the queens of Vikramaditya II, Lokamahadevi and Trailokya-mahadevi made grants and possibly consecrated the Lokesvara Temple (now Virupaksha temple) and also the Mallikarjuna temple respectively at Pattadakal.

4.1.2 Pallavas

On the downfall of the Satavahana power in the eastern part of the Peninsula, there rise the Ishvakus in the Krishna - Guntur region. The Ikshvakus were replaced by the Pallavas. The term Pallava means creeper and is a Sanskrit adaptation of the Tamil word tondai. The Pallavas were perhaps a local tribe who established their dominance in the Tondainadu. It however took them some time to become completely civilized and acceptable. The authority of the Pallavas extended over both southern Andhra and Northern Tamil Nadu. They set up their capital at Kanchi (modern Kanchipuram city in Tamil Nadu) which under them became a town of temples and vedic learning. The early Pallavas came into conflict with the Kadambas who had established their control over northern Karnataka and Konkan in the fourth century.

History of the Pallavas :

(1) Sivaskandavarman : The Prakrit charters mentions several early Pallavas king including Sivaskandavarman infact he was the first great ruler of the Pallava dynastry. He ruled in the 4th century A. D. He had extended his empire from the Krishna to south Penne and the Bellary District. He had also performed the horse (Asvamedha) sacrifice. His administration resembled the administrative system of the Mauryas.

(2) Vishnugopa : Sivaskandavarman was succeeded by Vishnugopa. An inscription at Allahabad reveals that he was one of the twelve Kings of Dakshnipatha defeated by Samudragupta. He ruled from 350 to 365 A.D.

(3) Simhavishnu : He ascended the throne probably in 565 A. D. In reality the glory of Pallava dynasty begins from him. He had high political ideas. He is credited with the conquest of Cholamandalam. He also defeated a number of enemies including the Cholas and the Kalabharas. He was also a great patron of literature. Bharavi the author of Kiratarjuniya belonged to his period. From the view-point

Mahabalipuram became highly important. At Mahabalipuram found the reliefs of Simhavishnu and his two queens.

(4) Mahendrawarman I : In the year 600 A.D. Simbhavishnu died and he was succeeded by his son Mahendravarman I. He was one of the greatest and the ablest of Pallavas. He had high standing titles as Chetthakari, Chirtrakarapulli, Mattavilasa and Vichitrachitra. During his reign the Pallava Chalukya war had begun. Pulakesin II the ruler of Chalukya dynasty was the invader. From Aihole inscription it is known that the Pallavas had obstructed the path of Pulakesin and consequently Pulakesin marched against the Pallavas. The Chalukya ruler after defeating the Pallavas occupied Vengi.

(5) Narsimhavarman I : Mahendravarman was succeeded by his son Narsimhavarman I. The latter ruled from about 630 to 668 A. D. He is regarded as the greatest king of the Pallava dynasty. His conquests bear testimony to his greatness. He had defeated Pulakesin II the Chalukya ruler in three battles. He was successful in capturing Vatapi the capital of Pulakesin II. The latter was himself killed. Narasimhavarman I took up the titles of Mahamalla and Vatapikonda or Captor of Vatapi. After the death of Pulakesin II Pallavas became all soverign in the Deccan. He is also said to have defeated the Cholas, the Cheras, the Pandyas and the Kalabhars. Narasimhavarman gave asylum to a Ceylonese prince Manavarman and sent two naval expenditions to Ceylon to help him to secure the throne of that country. In the first expedition he failed but in the second he was crowned with success. The details of this campaign are given in the Mahavamsa. It was during the reign of Narshimhavarman I that Pallava kingdom was visited by Hiuen Tsang. Hiuen Tsang visited Kanchi and has also given a lucid account of the Pallava dynasty. He writes that Kanchi had about 100 Buddists monasteries and more than 10,000 monks lived there. There were 80 Jain temples. The people loved learning. The soil of the country was fertile and there was an abundance of production. Hiuen Tsang says that Dharampala of the Nalanda university belonged to Kanchi.

Narsimhavarman I was one of the most powerful rulers of South Inida and raised the power and prestige of the Pallavas as far as Ceylon and South East Asia.

(6) Mahendravarman II : Narsimhavarman was succeeded by his son Mahendravarman II. He ruled for about 2 years from about 668 to 670 A. D. There is no significant event of his rule.

(7) Paramesvarvarman I : Mahendravarman II was succeeded by his son Paramesvaravarman I who ruled for about 670 to about 695

A. D. The old conflict with the Chalukyas started once again. Vikramaditya I the Chalukya ruler was successful against the Pallavas. The Chalukya were able to seize Kanchi. The Pallavas got a great reverse. It is to be noted that the Chalukya claim to victory is disputed in the Pallava record where it is stated that the Pallavas were victorious over the Chalukyas.

(8) Narsimhavarman II : After Paremesvaravarman I his son Narsimhavarman II came on the throne. He held the reins of administration from the 695 to 722 A. D. His period was a peaceful one he got erected a beautiful temple of Kalishnath near Kanchi and one at Mahabalipuram. It is believed that Dandin the great Sanskrit writer was his court-poet. He sent on ambassador to China. He was succeeded by his son Parmesvarvarman II. The latter ruled from about 722 to about 780 A.D. He had to face Chalukya invasion led by Yuvarja – Vikramaditya II.

(9) Nandivarman II : Nandivarman II was the next important king of the Pallava dynasty. We get an elaborate account of the work of Nandivarman II. He ruled from about 730 to about 800 A.D. During his rule the struggle between the Pallavas and the Chalukyas started once again. In 740 A.D. the Chalukya ruler Vikramaditya II had attacked the Pallavas and occupied Kanchi but Nandivarman succeeded in getting back Kanchi. Nandivarman had to fight against the Pandayas and Rashtrakutas. He is credited with the conquest of a part of Eastern Chalukyas territory. Though the Rashtrakuta ruler Dantidurga had established his authority over Kanchi but Nandivarman got it back by marrying his daughter Eeva to him. He was a follower of Vishnu and built the Muktesvara temple at Kanchi. Some other temples were also built by him. He gave great importance to religion and literature and himself was a great scholar. He also performed the Ashvamedha sacrifice. In 795 he was expired and was succeeded by his son Dantivarman.

(10) Dantivarman : Dantivarman succeeded his father Nandivarman. There were many other successors and the last of them was Aprajita Pallava. The latter defeated the Pandya king Varguna II in the battle of Sri-Purambiyam. But he himself was defeated by Aditya Chola towards the end of 9th century. From that time onward the Cholas became supreme and the Pallavas went into the background. During the period of decline the Pallavas had to fight against the Rashtrakutas. Govind II Rashtrakuta king levied tribute from the Pallavas. There were also wars between the Pallavas and the Gangas.

Pallava Society :

The Pallava period starting with Simhavishnu (575 AD – 900 AD) was a transitional stage. i.e. monument building, devotional (bhakti) sects of Alvars and Nayanars, rural Brahmanical institutions of Sanskrit learning, and the establishment of Chakravarti model of kingship over a territory of diverse people. While a system of ranked relationship among groups existed during the classical period, the Pallava period extolled ranked relationships based on ritual purity. Burton distinguishes between the Chakravati model and the Kshatriya model, and likes Kshatriyas to locally based warriors with ritual status sufficiently high enough to share with Brahmins; and states that in south India the Kshatriya model did not emerge.

4.1.3 Pandya

Sources of Pandya Rule :

(I) Sangam literature :

- Pandya history find mention in a number of poems in the Sangam literature. Among Nedunjeliyan II, and Mudukudimi Peruvaludi deserve special mention.
- Beside several short poetry found in the Akananuru and the Purananuru collections, there are two major works – Mathuraikkanci and the Netunalvatai – which give a glimpse into the society and commercial activities in the Pandya kingdom during the Sangam age.
- Silappatikaram mentions that the emblem of the Pandyas was that of a fish.

(II) Epigraphy :

- The earliest Pandya king to be found in epigraph is Nedunjeliyan, showed in the Tamil-Brahmi Mangulam inscription.
- Silver punch-marked coins with the fish symbol dating from around the same time have also been found.
- Pandyas also find mention in the pillars of Ashoka (273 – 232 BCE).
- Kharavela, the Kalinga king who ruled during the 2nd century BCE, claims to have acquired a large quantity of pearls from the Pandyas.

(III) Foreign sources :

- Pandyas had diplomatic relations as far as Rome is concerned.
- Megasthenes described in Indika as occupying the portion of India which lies southward and extends to the sea.
- The Periplus of the Erythraean Sea (c. 60 – c. 100 CE) describes the riches of a 'Pandian Kingdom' ("Pandi Mandala"):
- The country of the Pandyas was described as Pandya Mediterrane an and Modura Regia Pandionis by Ptolemy.
- Strabo states that an Indian king called Pandion sent Augustus Caesar "presents and gifts of honour".
- The Chinese historian Yu Huan in his 3rd-century text, the Weilüe, mentions the Panyue kingdom :
- In the later part of the 13th century Venetian traveller Marco Polo visited the Pandya kingdom and left a vivid description of the land and its people.

Tamil literary sources :

- Several Tamil literary works, such as Iraiyanar Agapporul, mention the legend of three separate Tamil Sangams lasting several centuries (before the Christian Era) and ascribe their patronage to the Pandyas.
- The Sangam poem Maduraikkanci by Mankudi Maruthanaar contains a description of Madurai and the Pandya country under the rule of Neduncheliyan III. The Nedunalvadai by Nakkirar gives a description of the king's palace.
- The Purananuru and Agananuru collections of the 3rd century BCE contain poems sung in praise of various Pandya kings.

Sanskrit literary sources :

- The Sanskrit grammarian Kātyāyana make references to the Pandya kingdom.
- The Arthashastra by Kautilya mentions pearls from Pandya kingdom and cotton textiles from Madurai.
- The Ramayana makes a few references to the Pandyas.
- Kalidasa's Raghuvamsha, an epic poem about Rama's dynasty, states that Ravana signed a peace treaty with a Pandya king.
- The Mahabharata mentions the Pandyas a number of times.

The Pandyas occupied the territory consisting of the modern districts of Madura and Tinnevelly part of Trichinopally and sometimes also of Travancore. During the period, of pliny the capital of the Pandyas was at Madura, although the kingdom had existed from much earlier days. The Pandyas were known to Katyayana the Sanskrit grammarian who flourished in the fourth century B.C. The writer of the Periplus of the Erythraean Sea (A.D. 80) and Ptolemy (A.D. 140) were well-informed about the names and positions of the marts and ports of the Pandya country.

History of the Pandyas :

(1) Nedum-Cheliyan : The ancient Tamil literature mentions many rulers who belonged to an extremely early period. However, the first Pandya King about whom some definite information can be given was Nedum-Cheliyan. He lived in the second century of the Christian era. It is important to note that a remarkable feature of the Pandya state at that time was the maintenance at Madura of a thriving literary academay or Sangam whose members produced literature of a very superior quality.

(2) Kudungon : It is not possible to write a connected history of the Pandya kingdom during the early centuries of the Christian era. Kudungon ruled from 590 to 620 A. D. Unfortunately we do not have any information about him. All that is known is that he suppressed the Kalabhras who had altogether overshadowed the Pandya realm before.

(3) Arikesary Marvarman : During his rule the Pandya power expanded at the cost of the Cheras. There also started the conflict between the Pandyas and the Pallavas. He was a brave and great soldier and he won a spectacular victory at Nelveli (Tinnevelly).

(4) Koccadiyan Ranadhira : Koccadiyan reduced an army Chief at Mardur ("a hill country between Tinnevelly and TravanCore"). He also conquered the Kongu country and assumed the title of Kongarkoman.

(5) Maravarman Raiasimha I : Maravarman succeeded his father Ranadhira. He had to carry on a prolonged war against the Pallavas. There was some problem in the Pallava kingdom on account of contender claim to the throne and Rajasimha I decided to avail of the chance. He took up the cause of Chitramaya who was claimant to the throne and went to war against the Pallavas. He start out very well and not only defeated the Pallava king but also besieged him at Nandipura. However, the situation changed very rapidly with the arrival of Udaychandra the Pallava general on the scene. The latter succeeded not only in saving Nandivarman but also was able to kill Chitramaya. In spite of this the Pandya power continued to grow. Rajasimha I was able to conquer Kongu country and beyond. He also claimed victory over the western Chalukyas of Badami.

(6) Vanguna I : Vanguna I who succeeded Rajasimha I ruled from 765 to 815 A.D He is known as the "greatest imperialist of his dynasty". During his rule the struggle between the Pandyas and the Pallavas started once again. The Pallava king entered into an coalition with the rulers of Kongu and Kerala but that did not help issues. The Pallvas were defeated at Pannagadam. Varguna also reduced the Army chief the Adigamas of Tagadur and the Kongu country. The outcome was that he became the sovereign "Lord of Tanjor, Tiruchirapalli, Salem and Coimbatore districts and also of Southern Travancore."

(7) Srimar Srivallabha : Srimar who succeeded his father Varguna I ruled from 815 to 862 A.D. He continued the aggressive policy of his father. He invaded Ceylon. In order to check the Pandya power a confederacy comprising of the Pallavas, Gangas, Magdhas, Cholas, Kalingas etc. was formed under the leadership of the Pallava ruler. However, the Pandya ruler was successful to defeat them all at Kundamukku (Kumbhakonam). The Pallavas tried once again and were able to defeat the Pandyas at Tellaru (near Wandiwash). It is important to note that the victory of Tellaru was a turning point and the Pandays were defeated once again by the son of Nandi the Pallava ruler.

(8) Varagunavarman II : Srimar was succeeded by his son Varagunavarman II and ruled from 862 to 880 A.D. He tried to enhanced the prestige of his dynasty by invading the Chola territory but he was surrounded by a joint army of the Pallavas, the Cholas and the Western Gangas. The united army was led by the Pallava ruler and the Pandyas were defeated at Sripurambiyam. It is rightly pointed out that this war ruined Varguna and the Pandya empire.

(9) Prantaka Viranayana : The brother of Varagunaverman II Prantaka Viranyana came at throne in 880 and ruled upto 900 A. D. and he was succeeded by his son Maravarman Rajasimha II who ruled from 900 to 920 A.D. The Cholas invaded the Pandya land whose ruler requested to the king of Ceylon for help but the joint armies of Ceylon and the Pandyas were defeated in 915 A.D. at Vellur. That put an end to independence of the Pandyas. Rajasimha ran away to Ceylon and after that took shelter in Kerala.

The Cholas over lordship was acknowledged by the Pandyas for 30 years. Fortunately for the Pandyas there was trouble in the Chola kingdom and Prantaka (the Chola king) was defeated by Krishna III the Rashtrakuta King in the battle fo Takkolam in 949 A. D. One Vira Pandya claims to have defeated the cholas Vira Pandya ruled as an independent ruler till he was killed by Aditya II. At the beginning of his rule Rajaraya Chola also defeated the Pandyas. His son Rajendra I attacked the Pandya territory and established a Chola-Pandya line by placing himself as the Viceroy with his headquarters at Madura. He was also successful to get back from the ruler of Ceylon the treasure and the insignia of the Pandya royalty. This happened after the ruler of Ceylon was defeated and captured. In the last quarter of 10th century and the beginning of the 11th century another effort was made by the Pandyas to revive their past glory but they failed on account of opposition from Kullotunga I who ruled from 1070 to 1120 A. D. Military colonies were also set up in the Pandya territory with a view to keep them in check.

The Pandays continued to grow during the 12th century. With the rulers of the Ceylon they carried on their struggle but the Pandyas received a set back as two rival claimants put forward their claims to the Pandya throne. Their names were Kulasekhar and Prakarma Pandya. The Cholas took up the cause of Kulasekhara while the ruler of Ceylon took up the cause of Prakarma Pandya. Kulasekhara was able to kill Prakarma Pandya and the army of Ceylon was defeated. The Cholas decided to teach a lesson to the ruler of Ceylon and the latter asked for the help of Kulasekhara by recognizing him as the rightful king of Pandyas. To reduce the power of Kulasekhara, Kullotunga sent an army under General Pallavarya. Pallavarya won a large number of victories over the Pandya King. He was finally captured and sent into exile. Vira-Pandya son of Prakarma Pandya was put on the Pandya throne. Vira Pandya joined the ruler of Ceylon against the Cholas but he was defeated and Vikrama Pandya came to the throne. Kullotunga III attacked once again the Pandya territory and overpowered Jatvarman Kulasekhara (1190-1226 A.D.) Sundara Pandya who ruled from 1226 to 1238 A. D. defeated Kullotunga III and he along with his son was driven into wilderness and Uraiyur and

Tanjore were burnt. By this victory was ushered into existence the glorious period of Pandya imperialism which remained intact throughout the 13th century."

(10) Sundara Pandya II : Sundara Pandya wsa succeeded by his son Sundara Pandya II. He was confronted with the rising power of the Hoyasalas of Dvarasmaudra who advanced along the base of the Eastern Ghats and annexed them. Only the coastline remained in the possession of the Pandyas. Finally the Pandyas became the feudatories of the Hoyasalas. When the Hoyasalas were defeated by the Muslims in the beginning of the 14th century, Pandya and the Madura territory came under the control of the Muslims. Petty Pandya chiefs continued to rule over Madura as Vassals first of the Muslim viceroys of the south and then of Vijayanagar empire which absorbed them in the 16th century.

Coinage :

- The earliest coins of Tamilakam bore the symbols of the Three Crowned Kings, the tiger, the fish and the bow.
- Symbols of the Cholas, Pandyas and Cheras. The coins bear the legend of different Pandya ruler in different times.
- Silver punch-marked and die struck copper coins was issued in the early period. A few gold coins were attributed to the Pandya rulers of this period, having image of fish, singly or in pairs etc.
- Some of the coins had the names Sundara, Sundara Pandya or merely the letter 'Su', coins bore a boar with the legend of 'Vira-Pandya.
- The coins were basically square, etched with elephant on one side. The inscription on the silver and gold coins during the Pandyas, were in Tamil-Brahmi and the copper coins bore the Tamil legends.
- The coins of the Pandyas, which has the fish symbols, were called 'Kodandaraman' and 'Kanchi' Valangum Perumal'.
- Apart from these, 'Ellamthalaiyanam' was seen on coins which had the standing king on one side and the fish on the other.
- 'Samarakolahalam' and 'Bhuvanekaviram' were found on the coins having a Garuda.
- 'Konerirayan' on coins having a bull and 'Kaliyugaraman' on coins that depict a pair of feet.

Trade :

- The Roman and Greek traders reached south India securing trade with the Tamil states of the Pandya, Chola and Chera dynasties.
- It helped in establishing trading settlements which secured trade with South Asia by the Greco-Roman world since the time of the Ptolemaic dynasty a few decades before the beginning of the Common Era and remained long after the fall of the Western Roman Empire.

Pearl fishing :

- Pearl fishing flourished during the Sangam age. The Pandya port city of Korkai was the center of pearl trade.
- Inferior quality of pearls that the Tamils did not require for their use was in very great demand in the foreign markets. Pearls were woven along with nice muslin cloth, before being exported. i.e. pearl from the Gulf of Mannar.
- The pearls from the Pandyan Kingdom were also in demand in the kingdoms of north India.
- The royal chariots were decked with pearls, as were the horses that dragged them.
- Pandyas derived great wealth from the pearl trade.

4.1.4 Struggle for Supremacy over Peninsular India

The principal interest in the political history of Peninsular India from the sixth to the eighth century centers around the long struggle for supremacy between the Pallavas of Kanchi and the Chalukya of Badami. The Pandyas who were in control of Madurai and Tirunelveli districts of Tamil Nadu joined this conflict as a poor third.

Although both the Pallavas and the Chalukyas championed Brahmanism, perfomed Vedic sacrifices and made grants to the Brahman as the two quarrelled with each other over plunder, prestige and territorial resources. Both tried to establish supremacy over the land lying between the Krishna and the Tungabhadra Time and again the Pallava princes tried to cross the Tunagabhadra which formed the natural historic boundary between many a kingdom of the Deccan and the deep south. The struggle continued over a long period with varying fortunes.

The first important event in this long conflict took place during the reign of Pulakesin II the most famous Chalukya king. He subjugated the Kadamba capital Vanavasi and compelled the Gangas of Mysore to acknowledge his suzerainty. He also defeated Harsha's army on the Narmada and checked his advance towards the Deccan. In his conflict with the Pallavas, he almost reached the Pallava capital but the Pallavas purchased peace by ceding their northern provinces to Pulakesin II. Around A. D. 610 Pulakesin II also conquered the entire area between the Krishna and the Godavari which came to be known as the province of Vengi. Here a branch of the main dynasty was set up and is known as the eastern Chalukyas of Vengi. However, Pulakesin's second invasion of Pallava territory ended in failure.

The Pallava king Narsimhavarman occupied the Chalukya capital Badami in about A.D. 642 when Pulakesin II was probably killed in a battle against the Pallavas. Narsimhavarman assumed the title of Vatapikonda or the conquerer of Vatapi. He is also said to have defeated the Cholas, the Cheras, the Pandyas and the Kalabhras towards the end of the seventh century there was a lull in this conflict which was again resumed in the first half of the eighth century. The Chalukya King Vikramaditya II is said to have overrun Kanchi three times. In A. D. 740 he completely routed the Pallavas. His victory ended the Pallavas supremacy in the far south although the ruling house continued for over a century thereafter. However, the Chalukyas were unable for long to enjoy the fruits of their victory over the Pallavas because their own hegemony was brought to an end in A.D. 757 by the Rashtrakutas.

4.2 RASHTRAKUTAS, PALAS, PRATIHARAS – TRIPARTITE STRUGGLE

After the disappearance of the centralized polities in northern India the period between 800-1200 A.D. saw the emgergence of regional kingdoms. Centralized states gave way to decentralized political system based on local interests. This change took place due to the emergence of a political economic structure termed as feudalism. Since the Gupta period the political structure in northern. India was increasingly becoming feudal. The outcome of the growth of feudalism was the carving out of independent principalities by the various vassals in different parts of the country. It is under these conditions that decentralized regional power flourished in the eighth-ninth century A. D. in northern India. This period is also known for the tripartite struggle between the Rashtrakutas, the Palas and the Pratiharas who established themselves in different regions.

4.2.1 Rashtrakutas

The Pallas and Pratiharas were ruling over eastern India and north India the Deccan was being ruled by the Rashtrakutas. The term 'Rashtrakutas' means designated officers in - charge of territorial divisions called Rashtras. The members of family were officers of Rashtra under the early Chalukyas of Badami. It is also believed that the Rashtrakutas were the descendants of 'Rata' and so they were named Rashtrakutas after 'Rata'.

Rise of Rashtrakutas Dantivarman or Dantidurga : He was the founder of the dynasty with his capital at Manyakhet or Malkhed near modern Solapur. He was ambitious and decided to take full advantage of the varied and valuable military experience he had gained in his campaigns in the north and south. He wiped out the Gurjara kingdom of Nandipuri and appointed his newphew Karaka to rule over the region. He led an expedition into Malava and by 750 A.D. he had became the master of central and southern Gujarat and the whole of Madhya Pradesh and Berar. He defeated Kirtivarman II the Chalukya king and thus by 753 A.D. he had became the master of the whole of Maharashtra. Krishna I was his successor.

Krishna I : He extended Rashtrakutas kingdom from Maharashtra to Karnataka. He defeated Kritivarman II the Chalukya ruler and thus the Chalukya empire was completely finished by about 760 A.D. He had than proceeded against the Gangas ruling in Mysore and occupied their capital. He also conquered Southern Konkan. The whole of the Marathi-speaking part of Madhya Pradesh came under the control of Krishna I.

Spread of Rashtrakuta Empire :

Govind II : Krishna I died about 773 A.D. and was succeded by his eldest son Govinda II. He had been nominated as Yuvraj by his father and had distinguished himself on the battlefield by defeating Vishnuvardhana IV of Vengi.

Dhruva : With the accession of Dhruva about A. D. 779 a new era began in the history of Rashtrakutas. The victories of Dhruva had made him the undisputed overlord of the entire Deccan. He was the first Rashtrakuta ruler to decisively intervene in the tripartite struggle being waged for the supremacy in north India and defeated both the Pratihara king Vatsaraja and Pala king Dharmapala.

Govinda III : Govinda III ascended the throne in 793 A.D. who also made incursions into north India and fought successfully against the palaking Dharmapala and Chakrayudha the puppet ruler of kanauj. In addition to the pratihara and Pala kings many more kings of Northern India were humbled by Govinda III however he reinstated them in their domininons. He also shattered the confederacy of the Ganga, Chera, Pandya and Pallava rulers in the south. He had installed a Siva temple at Kanchi to serve as a column of victory. The king of Ceylon was struck with fear of Govinda III and he also submitted to Govinda III.

Amoghavarsha I : Govinda III was succeeded by his son Amoghavarsha I. He ruled for 60 years. He is known better not for his martial spirit of his predecessor but for his learning towards religion and literature. The principles of Jainism appealed to him more however, this does not mean that he gave up his attrachment towards Hindusim. He was a liberal patron of literature and his court was adorned by a number of famous Hindu and Jain writers. He wrote a book of ethics called 'Kavirajamarga'.

Krishna II : Amonghavarsha I died about 878 A.D. and was succeeded by his son Krishna II who ruled for 36 years. Like his father he had learnings towards Jainism. It is claimed in many inscriptions that Krishan II terrified the Gurjaras, taught humility to Gaudas, destroyed the pride of Latas and his command was obeyed by the rulers of Anga, Ganga, Kalinga and Magadha. All this shows that most of the time of Krishna II was spent in wars.

Wars with Bhoja : The most arduous of his campaigns were those against the Pratiharas and the eastern Chalukyas. He had to fight with the Gurjara – Pratihara ruler Bhoja.

War with the Eastern Chalukyas : The war with the eastern Chalukyas was a more serious affair and at one time even threatened the very existence of the Rashtrakuta kingdom.

Relations with Cholas : Krishna II seems to have political relations with the Cholas. One of his daughter was married to the

Chola King, Aditya I and there was a son by this marriage, named Kannara. Krishna II invaded the Chola kingdom in order to put his grandson on the throne. However he was defeated.

Indra III : Krishna II was succeed by his grandson Indra III. He had inherited the military dash and daring of Govinda III. He renewed the war against the Pratiharas. He defeated the Pratihara king Mahipala I and plundered his capital Kanauj. The capture of Kanauj was a very great achievement for the Rashtrakutas. The Rashtrakutas also fought war against Vengi during the reign of Indra III but there was not much success on either side.

Govinda IV : Govinda was a young man of about 25 at the time of his accession and soon gave himself up to life of vicious pleasures. His administration became tyrannical and unpopular and his ministers and feudatories felt that his removal was necessary in the interests of the empire.

Krishna III : Krishna III succeeded to throne on his father Amoghavarsha II death towards the end of 939 A.D. He was the last in line of brilliant rulers of Rashtrakutas. He was engaged in a struggle against the Paramaras of Malwa and eastern Chalukya of Vengi. He also launched a campaign against the Chola ruler of Tanjore and his armies reached Rameshwaram where he built a pillar of victory and a temple.

Krishna III was one of the ablest monarch of the Rashtrakuta dynasty. He was not as successful in his northern campaigns as Dhruva and Govinda III. But there is no doubt that unlike any of his predecessor he was the lord of the whole of Deccan. Krishna was in effective possession of a large part of the Chola kingdom.

Khottiga : Krishna III apparently had no issue living at the time of his death. Since he was succeeded by his younger brother khottiga. The new ruler was an old man at the time of his accession and seems to have lacked military capacity. No wonder he was not able to meet the invasion of his kingdom by the Parmara king named Siyaka. The latter was successful in capturing and plundering Malkhed the capital of the Rashtrakutas in 972 A.D. This was too much for Khottiga who died broken-hearted in September 972 A.D.

Karka II : Karka II succeeded khottiga. The prestige of the empire was already gone and the new ruler worsened the situation by bad administration. Taila II who was feudatory of the Rashtrakutas made preparations against the new king and revolted in the end of 973 A.D. Karka II was defeated and managed to run away. Efforts were made to reestablish the Rashtrakutas but all those were put in vain and by 975 A.D. Taila became the master of the Deccan.

Thus it was after a vigorous career of almost two centuries and a quarter the imperial Rashtrakutas disappeared from history.

(I) Administration :

- The Rashtrakutas selected the crown and prince based on heredity. The crown did not always pass on to the eldest son.
- The most important position under the king was the Chief Minister (Mahasandhivigrahi).
- Under him was the commander (Dandanayaka), the foreign minister (Mahakshapataladhikrita) and a prime minister (Mahamatya or Purnamathya), all of whom were usually associated with one of the feudatory kings.
- A Mahasamantha was a feudatory or higher ranking regal officer. All cabinet ministers were well versed in political science (Rajneeti) and possessed military training.
- The kingdom was divided into Mandala or Rashtras (provinces). A Rashtra was ruled by a Rashtrapathi who on occasion was the emperor himself.
- Under a Rashtra was a Vishaya (district) overseen by a Vishayapathi.
- Below the Vishaya was the Nadu looked after by the Nadugowda sometimes there were two such officials, one assuming the position through heredity and another appointed centrally.
- The lowest was Grama or village administered by a Gramapathi or Prabhu Gavunda.
- The Rashtrakuta army was made of large contingents of infantry, horsemen, and elephants. A standing army was always ready for war in a cantonment in the regal capital of Manyakheta.
- The feudatory kings were expected to contribute to the defense of the empire in case of war. Chieftains and all the officials also served as commanders.
- The Rashtrakutas issued coins (minted in an Akkashale) such as Suvarna, Drammas in silver and gold, Kalanju, Gadyanaka, Kasu, Manjati and Akkam.

(II) Economy :

- The Rashtrakuta economy sustained on its natural and agricultural produce, its manufacturing revenues and gains from its conquests.
- Cotton was the main crop of the regions of southern Gujarat, Khandesh and Berar. Minnagar, Gujarat, Ujjain, Paithan and Tagara became important centres of textile industry.
- Muslin cloth was manufactured in Paithan and Warangal. The cotton yarn and cloth was exported from Bharoch.
- White calicos were manufactured in Burhanpur and Berar and exported to Persia, Turkey, Poland, Arabia and Egypt.
- In the Konkan region, large quantities of betel leaves, coconut and rice were produced while the lush forests of Mysore, produced sandal, timber, teak and ebony.
- Incense and perfumes were exported from the ports of Thana and Saimur.
- The Deccan was rich in minerals i.e. the copper mines of Cudappah, Bellary, Chanda, Buldhana, Narsingpur, Ahmadnagar, Bijapur and Dharwar were important source of income.
- Diamonds were mined in Cudappah, Bellary, Kurnool and Golconda; the capital Manyakheta and Devagiri were important diamond and jewellery trading centres.
- The leather industry and tanning flourished in Gujarat and some regions of northern Maharashtra.
- Mysore with its vast elephant herds was important for the ivory industry.
- The Rashtrakuta empire controlled most of the western sea board of the subcontinent which facilitated its maritime trade.
- Port of Bharoch was one of the most prominent ports in the world at that time. The empire's main exports were cotton yarn, cotton cloth, muslins, hides, mats, indigo, incense, perfumes, betel nuts, coconuts, sandal, teak, timber, sesame oil and ivory.
- Its major imports were pearls, gold, dates from Arabia, slaves, Italian wines, tin, lead, topaz, storax, sweet clover, flint glass, antimony, gold and silver coins, singing boys and girls from other lands.
- Trading in horses was an important and profitable business, monopolised by the Arabs and some local merchants.
- The Rashtrakuta government levied a shipping tax of one golden Gadyanaka on all foreign vessels.

- Artists and craftsman formed corporations (guilds) rather than as individual business. i.e. weavers, oilmen, artisans, basket and mat makers and fruit sellers.
- The government's income came from regular taxes, occasional taxes, fines, income taxes, miscellaneous taxes and tributes from feudatories.
- Income tax included taxes on crown land, wasteland, specific types of trees considered valuable to the economy, mines, salt, treasures unearthed by prospectors.
- Additionally, customary presents were given to the king or royal officers.
- The land owner or tenant paid a variety of taxes, including land taxes, produce taxes and payment of the overhead for maintenance of the Gavunda (village head).
- In most of the kingdom, land taxes were paid in goods and services and rarely in cash.
- A portion of all taxes earned by the government was returned to the villages for maintenance.
- Taxes were levied on potters, sheep herders, weavers, oilmen, shopkeepers, stall owners, brewers and gardeners.
- Taxes were levied on perishable items such as fish, meat, honey, medicine, fruits and essentials like fuel. Taxes on salt and minerals were mandatory.
- The state claimed all such properties whose deceased legal owner had no immediate family to make an inheritance claim.
- Other taxes included ferry and house taxes.

Society :

- Chronicles mention more castes than the four commonly known castes some as many as seven castes.
- According to Al-Biruni, there were sixteen castes including the four basic castes of Brahmins, Kshatriya, Vaishya and Sudras.
- The Zakaya or Lahud caste consisted of communities specialising in dance and acrobatics.
- The Antyajas caste provided many menial services to the wealthy.
- Brahmins enjoyed the highest status in Rashtrakuta society; only those Kshatriyas in the Sat-Kshatriya sub-caste (noble Kshatriyas) were higher in status.

- The occupations of Brahmins usually related to education, the judiciary, astrology, mathematics, poetry and philosophy or the occupation of hereditary administrative posts.
- By the 9th century, kings belonging to all the four castes had achieved the highest seat in the monarchical system in Hindu India.
- Landownership by people of all castes is recorded in inscriptions.
- Intercaste marriages in the higher castes were only between highly placed Kshatriya girls and Brahmin boys, but was relatively frequent among other castes.
- Intercaste functions were not encourages and dining together between people of various castes was avoided.
- Joint families were the norm and women and daughters had rights over property and land.
- The arranged marriage system followed a strict policy of early marriage for women.
- Sati (a custom in which a dead man's widow would immolate herself on her husband's funeral pyre) rare, was practiced but were rare widows were allowed to grow their hair but decorating it was discouraged.
- The remarriage of a widow was rare among the upper castes and more accepted among the lower castes.
- Men wore a loose garment on top and a garment worn like a dhoti for the lower part of the body. Only kings could wear turbans.
- Dancing was a popular entertainment and often present in temples.
- Other recreational activities included attending animal fights of the same or different species.
- Astronomy and astrology were well developed as subjects of study, and there were many superstitious beliefs such as catching a snake alive proved a woman's chastity.

4.2.2 Palas

Rise of the Palas :

There was anarchy and confusion for more than a century in Bengal after the death of Sasanka the famous Gauda ruler. Thus the history of Bengal from the death of Sasanka and Harsha up to the ascendancy of the Palas remains in obsecure. At this time West Bengal was known as Gauda and East Bengal as Venga. Bengal was subject to internal disorder. This lead to a revolution and a result of this the people selected a person named Gopala as their ruler and there by put an end to the Chaos in the country in 750 A.D. We do not posses many details about the career of Gopala. However he introduced peace in the Kingdom and laid the foundation for the great future for his family known as the Pala dynasty.

History of The Palas :

Dharmapala : Gopala was succeeded by his son Dharmapala about A.D. 780. He ruled for about 40 years. He was a man of dynamatic personality and found himself in a position to undertake the expansion of his empire. He defeated Indrayudha the king of Kanauj and installed Chakrayudha to the throne of Kanauj. After this victory Dharmapala held a Durbar at Kanauj. This Darbar was attended by a large number of kings. But Dharmapala could not consolidate his position. Rashtrakuta king Dhruva could not tolerate the imperial pretensions of Dharmapala and routed him in a battle. Vatsaraja the Pratihara ruler too defeated Dharmapala but he himself was defeated by Rashtrakuta king Dhruva. After defeating Dharmapala, Dhruva went back to the Deccan. It is rightly contended that Dharmapala did not lose much while the Pratihara dynasty lost heavily. After Dhruva's depature Dharmapala took full advantage of the situation and by a series of victorious campaigns made himself the lord of practically the whole of Northern India. Mean while the Pratihara power revived under Nagabhatta II. He defeated Dharmapala near Monghyr. However Nagabhatta II was himself defeated by Govinda III the Rashtrakuta ruler. But after this victory Govinda III left for the Deccan and thus Northern India became a free field for the military aspiration of Dharmapala. He remained a powerful ruler till the end of his life. Dharmapala was a great patron of Buddhism and founded the famous Buddhist monastery at Vikramashila.

Devapala : Dharmapala was succeeded by his son Devapala who is justifiedly counted as the most powerful Pala ruler. He not only maintained intact the territories inherited by him from his father but also added to them. He conquered Assam and also Orissa (today's Odisha). The Pala also ruled over Bihar and Bengal with many vicissitudes of fortune for over four centuries. It appears that Devapala defeated. Amonghavarsha the Rastrakuta ruler.

Devapala invaded the kingdom of Ramabhadra the Pratihara king who was a son of Nagabhatta II. Ramabhadra was defeated by Devapala. Devapala also defeated king Bhoja. Devapala had to fight against three generations of the Pratihara rulers and in spite of difficulties he was able to maintain his supremacy in Northern India.

Vigrahapala to Vigrahapala II : Devapala was succeeded by Vigrahapala. He ruled for about 3 or 4 years. After that he abdicated and began to live the life of an ascetic.

Vigrahapala was succeeded by Narayanapala. He was a man of pacific and religious disposition. Sometime after 860 A.D. the Rashtrakutas defeated the Palas. The Pratiharas took advantage of this and extended their power to the east. The Palas lost South Bihar. For some time even North Bengal came into the hands of the Pratiharas. The successes of the Pratiharas weakened all the more the Palas. The subordinate chiefs under the Palas revolted. However Narayanapala is stated to have recovered North Bengal and South Bihar form the Pratiharas about the year 908 A.D. This was done after the defeat of the Pratiharas by the Rashtrakutas under their king krishna II. Before his death Narayanapala was able to establish his supremacy in Bengal and Bihar. Narayanapala was succeeded by Rajyapala. The latter was succeeded by Gopala II and Vigrahapala II. They all covered a period of about 80 years.

Mahipala I : Vigrahapala II was succeeded by his son Mahipala I. The Pala power was once again revived under him. The most important event of the rule of Mahipala was the invasion of the North by king Rajendra Chola. Though Rajendra Chola defeated king Mahipala, Mahipala was successful in checking the advance of Rajendra Chola beyond the Gangas. The territories of Mahipala have suffered during the later part of his reign. Mahipala was succeeded by his son Nayapala who was successful in defeating Karna the Kalachuri ruler who wish to expand his territory at the cost of the Palas. Nayapala was succeeded by his son Vigrahapala III. Karna the Kalachuri king once again invaded Gauda but he himself was defeated. Vigrahapala was succeeded by Mahipal II.

Mahipala II : It was during the reign of Mahipala II that his feudatories became powerful and they came together by defeating Mahipala II and killed him.

Rampala : During the reign of Ramapala many rebellious feudatories started taking advantage of the misfortunes of the palas. Ramapala visited them personally and by his tact and cleverness won them over. He was able to recover his paternal dominions in Northern Bengal and after that overran Kalinga and Kamarupa.

Successors of Ramapala : He was succeeded by his son Kumarapala. These was a revolt in his reign in Kamarupa which was quelled by his minister Vaidyadeva who himself became virtually independent in Kamrupa. The successors of Kumarapala were weak and consequently they could not arrest the decline of the dynasty. The feudatory chiefs began to assert their independence. The authority of the Palas was confined to only a portion of Bihar.

The last Pala king about whom we know anything was Govindapala. Thus, it was the Pala dynasty which at one time rose to the rank of the foremost imperial rulers of India lost its sovereign power after a rule of nearly 400 years.

(I) Administration :

- The Pala rule was monarchical and the king was the centre of all power. Pala kings would adopt imperial titles like Parameshwara, Paramvattaraka, Maharajadhiraja. Pala kings appointed Prime Ministers. The Gargas served as the Prime Ministers of the Palas for 100 years.
- Pala Empire was divided into separate *'Bhuktis'* (Provinces). Bhuktis were divided into *'Vishayas'* (Divisions) and **'Mandalas'** (Districts).
- Smaller units were *'Khandala', 'Bhaga', 'Avritti',* Chaturaka, and Pattaka. Administration covered widespread area from the grass root level to the imperial court.

4.2.3 Pratiharas and Parmaras

Pratiharas :

The early history of Gurjara pratiharas is shrouded in enigma. According to some historians they came to India from the central Asian region after the Gupta period and they settled in Rajashtan step by step they gathered political importance. But the bardic tradition of Rajasthan claims that the Gurjara pratiharas were born our of a yajna done at Mount Abu. Others born out of his yajna were Chalukyas, Parmaras and Chahmanas. It is further argue that these four dynasties of Rajputs were created for the protection of the country from external aggressions. The Pratiharas ague that they were called Pratihara (literary means door keeper) because their ancestor Lakshmana served as a door keeper to his brother Rama. The geographical name of Gujarat is derived from Gurjara.

History of the Pratiharas : The early history of the pratiharas is saved in the Gwalior inscription of Bhoja the seventh and the most famous king of the dynasty. This dynasty was founded by Harichandra in 6th century A.D. and remained influential till 11th century A.D.

Nagabhatta I : Nagabhatta I was the real founder of the fame of family and the first important ruler of this dynasty. He ruled from 730 A.D. to 756 A.D. His kingdom included Gwalior, Bharuch and Malwa Awani was the capital of his kingdom. He defeated the Arab Commander Junaid and his successor Tamin in the battle of Rajastan and successfully defended the western frontiers against Arab invasion.

Vatsaraja : Vatsaraja who succeeded Nagabhatta I captured Kanauj from the Pala king Dharmapala but unfortunately the fruits of his victory were grabed away from him by the Rashtrakuta king Dhruva who defeated Vatsaraja. Dharmapala took advantage of the reverse of Vatsaraja and set up his own candidate Chakrayudha on the throne of Kanauj.

Nagabhatta II : Nagabhatta II succeeded vatsaraja around 805 A.D. who was the son of Vatsaraja and the most illustrious king of Gurjara pratihara dynasty. He made an alliance with various other states especially with Andhra, Kalinga and Vidharbha. He made extensive preparation and fought against his rivals. He first defeated Chakrayudha and captured Kanauj. Then he defeated Dharmapala and fought with Rashtrakuta king Govinda III. It is also stated that Nagabhatta II defeated sultan Vega who was the son of the governor of Sind unde the caliph-Al-Mamun. Nagabhatta II is known for rebuilding the Somnath Temple in 815 A.D. Which was destroyed by Arab armies of Junaid in 725 A.D.

Ramabhadra : Ramabhadra succeeded his father Nagabhatta II during his brief reign of three years the Pratihara suffered most owing to the aggressive policy of the Pala King Devapala.

Bhoja I : About A.D. 836 Bhoja I succeeded his father Ramabhadra. Bhoja I within a few years of his accession succeeded in restoring the falling fortunes of his dynasty. The death of Devapala followed by the Rahtrakutas invasion of Bengal must have provided a golden apportunity to the Pratihara king. In another way luck also favoured Bhoja I. The Rashtrakuta king Krishna II was engaged in a life and death struggle with the Eastern Chalukyas. Bhoja I defeated Krishna II and captured the reign of Gujarat and Malwa. After asserting victory over the two big rivals, Bhoja I has no trouble in establishing his Sovereignity over the Avadh, Punjab and other regions of north India and consolidated his empire.

The name of Bhoja is famous in many legends. He was the devotee of Vishnu and adopted the title of Adivaraha which has been inscribed in some of his coins. He is also known as 'Prabhasa' and 'Mihir'. Around A.D. 851 an assessment of Bhoja as a conqueror and administrator is given by the Arab historian sulaiman. He wrote that Bhoja kept numerous forces and no other Indian king had such fine cavalry. He has got riches and his horses and camels are numerous. In his states exchanges are carried on with gold and silver. There is no other country in Indian more secure from robbers.

Mahendrapala I : About A.D. 885 Bhoja I was succeeded by his son Mahendrapala I. Mahendrapala I not only kept the huge empire intact but even extended his boundaries. The Pratihara empire now stretched almost from the Himalayas in the north to the Vindhyas in the south and from Bengal in the east to Gujarat in the West. He was also known as 'Nibhayanarendra' and 'Mahendrayudha'. He was a liberal supporter of learned man. His guru Rajashekhara occupies a distinguished position in the Indian literature. His works include Haravilasa, Bala Bharata, Bala - Ramayana, Bhuvanakosha, Karpuramanjari and Kavyamimansa.

For over two hundred years from the eighth century to the tenth century A.D. the pratiharas dominated North India. In A.D. 915-916 Al-Masudia native of Baghdad who visited India attested to the great powers and prestige of the Pratihara rulers and the vastness of their empire. He says that empire of pratiharas had 1,800,000 villages, the cities and rural areas were about 2000 km in length and 2000 km in breadth. The king's army had four divisions each compriseing of 7,00,000 to 9,00,000 men.

Between A.D. 915 and A.D. 918 the Rashtrakuta king. Indra III again attacked Kanauj leaving it completely ravaged. This hurt the pratihara empire. Krishna III the another Rashtrakuta ruler invaded north India in about A.D. 963 and defeated the pratihara rulers. This was followed by the decline of pratihara empire.

Parmaras Empire :

The Paramara dynasty ruled Malwa and surrounding areas in west-central India between 9th and 14th centuries.

- 10th century ruler Siyaka, was a vassal of the Rashtrakutas of Manyakheta.
- Around 972 CE, Siyaka sacked the Rashtrakuta capital Manyakheta, and established the Paramaras as a sovereign power.
- The Malwa region become the core Paramara territory, with Dhara (now Dhar) as their capital.
- The dynasty reached its zenith under Bhoja, whose kingdom extended from Chittor in the north to Konkan in the south, and from the Sabarmati River in the west to Vidisha in the east.
- The Paramara faced conflicts with the Chaulukyas of Gujarat, the Chalukyas of Kalyani, the Kalachuris of Tripuri and other neighbouring kingdoms.
- The later Paramara rulers moved their capital to Mandapa-Durga after Dhara was sacked many times by their enemies.
- Mahalakadeva, the last known Paramara king, was defeated and killed by the forces of Alauddin Khalji of Delhi in 1305 CE.

Conflicts :

- As already mentioned the first independent king of the Paramara dynasty was Siyaka
- Siyaka was a feudatory of the Rashtrakuta ruler Krishna III in his early days.
- As a Rashtrakuta feudatory, Siyaka war part of their campaigns against the Pratiharas.
- He also defeated some Huna chiefs ruling to the north of Malwa.
- After the death of Krishna III, Siyaka defeated his successor Khottiga in a battle socked the Rashtrakuta capital Manyakheta.
- Munja Siyaka's successor achieved victories against the Chahamanas of Shakambari, the Chahamanas of Naddula, the Guhilas of Mewar, the Hunas, the Kalachuris of Tripuri, and the ruler of Gurjara region.
- He also achieved some early victories against the Western Chalukya king Tailapa II, but was ultimately defeated and killed by Tailapa some time between 994 CE and 998 CE.

- As a consequence of this defeat, the Paramaras lost their southern territories to the Chalukyas.
- Munja rule attracted scholars from different parts of India to Malwa. He was also a poet himself.
- Munja's brother Sindhuraja (990s CE) defeated the Western Chalukya king Satyashraya, and recovered the territories lost to Tailapa II.
- He also defeated a Huna chief, the Somavanshi of south Kosala, the Shilaharas of Konkana, and the ruler of Lata.
- Sindhuraja's son Bhoja is the most famous ruler of the Paramara dynasty.
- Around 1018 CE, he defeated the Chalukyas of Lata.
- Between 1018 CE and 1020 CE, he gained control of the northern Konkan, whose Shilahara rulers probably became his feudatories.
- Bhoja formed an alliance against the Kalyani Chalukya king Jayasimha II, with Rajendra Chola and Gangeya-deva Kalachuri.
- During the last years of Bhoja's reign, sometime after 1042 CE, Jayasimha's son and successor Someshvara I invaded Malwa, and sacked his capital Dhara.
- Although Bhoja re-established his control over Malwa soon after the departure of the Chalukya army, but the defeat pushed back the southern boundary of his kingdom from Godavari to Narmada.
- Bhoja's efforts to expand his kingdom eastwards was defeated by the Chandela king Vidyadhara.
- Bhoja also launched a campaign against the Kachchhapaghatas of Gwalior, but his attacks were repulsed by their ruler Kirtiraja.
- Bhoja defeated the Chahamanas of Shakambhari, killing their ruler Viryarama.
- During the last year of Bhoja's reign, or shortly after his death, the Chaulukya king Bhima I and the Kalachuri king Karna attacked his kingdom.
- At its peak, Bhoja's kingdom extended from Chittor in the north to upper Konkan in the south, and from the Sabarmati River in the west to Vidisha in the east.
- His major claim to fame was his reputation as a scholar-king, who patronized arts, literature and sciences. Noted poets and writers of his time sought his sponsorship.

- Bhoja was himself a scholar, whose writings cover a wide variety of topics include grammar, poetry, architecture, yoga, and chemistry.
- Bhoja established the Bhoj Shala which was a centre for Sanskrit studies and a temple of Sarasvati in present-day Dhar.
- The Bhojeshwar Temple, the construction of three now-breached dams is attributed to him.

Decline of the Parmar empire :

- Bhoja's successor Jayasimha I, faced the joint Kalachuri-Chaulukya invasion immediately after Bhoja's death.
- Jayasimha's successor and Bhoja's brother Udayaditya was defeated by Chamundaraja, his vassal at Vagada.
- He repulsed an invasion by the Chaulukya ruler Karna, with help from his allies. Udayaditya's eldest son Lakshmadeva has been credited with extensive military conquests.
- Udayaditya's younger son Naravarman faced several defeats, losing to the Chandelas of Jejakabhukti and the Chaulukya king Jayasimha Siddharaja.
- By the end of his reign, Vijayapala had created an independent kingdom to the north-east of Ujjain.
- Yashovarman lost control of the Paramara capital Dhara to Jayasimha Siddharaja.
- His successor Jayavarman I regained control of Dhara, but soon lost it to an usurper named Ballala.
- A branch of the Paramaras, (Mahakumaras), ruled the area around Bhopal during this time.
- Nearly two decades later, Jayavarman's son Vindhyavar-man defeated the Chaulukya king Mularaja II, and re-established the Paramara sovereignty in Malwa.
- Malwa faced repeated invasions from the Hoysalas and the Yadavas of Devagiri during the rule.
- He was also defeated by the Chaulukya general Kumara. Even then he was able to restore the Paramara power in Malwa before his death.
- Vindhyavarman's son Subhatavarman invaded Gujarat, and plundered the Chaulukya territories, but he was ultimately forced to retreat.

- His son Arjunavarman I also invaded Gujarat, and defeated Jayanta-simha, who had usurped the Chaulukya throne for a brief period.
- He was defeated by Yadava general Kholeshvara in Lata.
- Arjunavarman is successor Devapala, continued to face struggles against the Chaulukyas and the Yadavas.
- The Sultan of Delhi Iltutmish captured Bhilsa during 1233-34 CE, but Devapala defeated the Sultanate's governor and regained control of Bhilsa.
- According to the Hammira Mahakavya, he was killed by Vagabhata of Ranthambhor, who suspected him of plotting his murder in connivance with the Delhi Sultan.
- During the rule of Devapala's son Jaitugideva, the power of the Paramaras greatly reduced because of invasions from the Yadava king Krishna, the Delhi Sultan Balban, and the Vaghela prince Visala-deva.
- Devapala's younger son Jayavarman II also faced attacks from these three powers.
- Arjunavarman II, the successor of Jayavarman II, proved to be a weak ruler. In the 1270s, the Yadava ruler Ramachandra invaded Malwa, and in the 1280s, the Ranthambhor Chahamana ruler Hammira also raided Malwa.
- Arjuna's successor Bhoja II also faced an invasion from Hammira.
- Mahalakadeva, the last known Paramara king, was defeated and killed by the forces of Alauddin Khalji in 1305 CE.

4.2.4 Tripartite Struggle

Tripartite Struggle :

As mentioned above makes it quite open that towards the close of the eight century A.D. there were three great powers in India. The Rashtrakutas in the Deccan, the Palas in the east and the Gurjara pratihara in the north emerged as powerful dynasties almost at the same time. The tripartite struggle for the supremacy between the Rashtrakutas, the palas and the Gurjara pratihara was the important event of these centuries.

It is said that the chief reason for this battle was the desire to possess the city of Kanauj which was then a sign of sovereignty another reason was to control the intermediate fertile regions. It must also kept in mind about these three powers that their military equipment, administrative machinery and the strategic concepts were all more or less the same. The Arab travellers also proves that these powers were same strength. Due to this balance of power there was a great deal of political stability within the regions which encouraged the development education and culture.

The first clash took place among the Rashtrakutas king Dhruva, the pala king Dharmapala and the pratihara king Vatsaraja. In the first stage Rashtrakuras attained a complete victory but the death of Dhuva proved to be a setback to Rashtrakutas. In the second stage pala king Devapala was the most outstanding because his contemporaty Rashtrakuta and Pratihara kings were weak rulers. However the ninth century the pratihara king Bhoja and Mahendrapala proved to be more mighty than their contemporaries of the other two dynasties. The Rashtrakutas once again acquired the strength towards the end of the ninth century under their kings Indra III and Krishna III. Whose power was felt not only in the north but also in the south.

Around the end of the tenth century A.D. the powers of Rashtrakutas, pala and pratiharas declined at the same time. The end of these three dynasties marked the end of the brilliant epoch of more than three hundred years.

4.3 Literature, Religion, Art and Architecture

In the previous chapter we had a glance of the gripping panorama of events which unfolded during a span of seven hundred years. Dynasties may appear and disappear on the sand of time. But when our attention turns away from these clashes of arms we find the splendours of time. These splendours include literature, religion art and architecture.

4.3.1 Literature

Literature :

Chalukyas the Aihole inscription of Pulakeshin II Sanskrit language and Kannada script is a classical piece of poetry. A few verses by Vijayanaka have been preserved. Famous writers in Sanskrit from the Western Chalukya period are Vijnaneshwara who Mitakshara, a book on Hindu law, and King Someshvara III, a noted scholar, compiled an encyclopedia of all arts and sciences called Manasollasa. Inscriptions refer to Kannada as the "natural language". The Kappe Aryabhatta record of c. 700 in tripadi is the earliest available work in Kannada Poetry. Karnateshwara Katha, is believed to be a eulogy of Pulakeshin II and to have belonged to this period. Other probable Kannada writers, whose works are not extant now but titles of which are known from independent references are Syamakundacharya (Prabhrita), and Srivaradhadeva (Chudamani) etc. The rule of the Western and Eastern Chalukyas, however, is a major event in the history of Kannada and Telugu literatures respectively. The "three gems" of Kannada literature, Adikavi Pampa, Sri Ponna and Ranna belonged to this period. During the 11th century, Telugu literature was born under the patronage of the Eastern Chalukyas with Bhatta as its first writer.

Pallavs :

During the reign of the Pallavas, there was a lot of literary activity. Dandin was the court-poet of Narasimhavarman II. Excepting a few inscriptions at the beginning the rest of the inscriptions of Pallavas were writing in Sanskrit. In the South, Kanchi was the seat of Sanskrit learning. The Brahmanas paid special attention to the study of Sanskrit. The works of Kalidas, Bharavi and Varahamihira were well - known in the country. A provision was made for the recitation of the Mahabharata in a Mandapa at Kurram near Kanchi. There were 108 families which were completely devoted at that place to the study of the Vedas. The Tamil Kural of Trivalluvar was a work of great learning. Mattavilasa Prahasana (the Delight of the Drunkards) was written by the pallava king Mahendravarman I in Sanskrit. Mahendravarman I was a versatile genius. He was both a poet and a singer.

Rashtrakutas :

Kannada became more prominent literary language during the Rashtrakuta rule. It's script and literature showed remarkable growth, and productivity. This period marked the end of the classical Prakrit and Sanskrit era. Court poets and royalty created eminent works in Kannada and Sanskrit that included prose, poetry, rhetoric, the Hindu epics and the life history of Jain tirthankars. Writers such as Asaga gained fame, and noted scholars such as the Mahaviracharya wrote on pure mathematics. Kavirajamarga (850) by King Amoghavarsha I is the earliest available book on rhetoric and poetics in Kannada. The Jain writer Adikavi Pampa, one of the most influential Kannada writers, became famous for Adipurana (941), other notable work was Vikramarjuna Vijaya (941). Another notable Jain writer in Kannada was Sri Ponna, patronised by King Krishna III and famed for Shantipurana. His other writings in Kannada were Bhuvanaika-ramaabhyudaya, Jinaksharamale and Gatapratyagata. Adikavi Pampa and Sri Ponna are called "gems of Kannada literature". Important mathematical theories and axioms were postulated by Mahaviracharya. His greatest contribution was Ganitasarasangraha, a writing in 9 chapters. Somadevasuri of 950 wrote in the court of Arikesari II, a feudatory of Rashtrakuta Krishna III in Vemulavada. He was the author of Yasastilaka champu, Nitivakyamrita and other writings. Ugraditya, a Jain ascetic from Hanasoge in the modern Mysore district wrote a medical treatise called Kalyanakaraka. Trivikrama a noted scholar in the court of King Indra III. wrote Nalachampu (915). Damayanti Katha, Madala-sachampu and Begumra plates. A Jinasenai contributions are Dhavala and Jayadhavala. Other contributions from Jinasena were Adipurana, later completed by his disciple Gunabhadra, Harivamsha and Parshvabhyudaya.

Language (Rashtrakutas) :

The royal courts of peninsular India (outside Tamilakam) interfaced between the increasing use of the local Kannada language and the expanding Sanskritic culture. Inscriptions, demonstrate the use of Kannada as the primary language along with Sanskrit. The local language formed the desi (popular) literature while literature in Sanskrit was more marga (formal). Educational institutions and places of higher learning (ghatikas) taught in Sanskrit, Kannada increasingly became the speech of personal expression of devotional closeness of a worshipper to a private deity. The patronage Kannada received from rich and literate Jains led to its use in the devotional movements of later centuries. Kannada was not only popular in the modern Karnataka region but had spread further north into present day southern Maharashtra and to the northern Deccan by the 8th

century. Kavirajamarga, the work on poetics, refers to the entire region between the Kaveri River and the Godavari River as "Kannada country". Higher education in Sanskrit included the subjects of Veda, Vyakarana (grammar), Jyotisha (astrology), Sahitya (literature), Mimansa (Exegesis), Dharmashastra (law), Puranas (ritual), and Nyaya (logic law). Trivikrama's Sanskrit writing, Nalachampu, is perhaps the earliest in the champu style from the Deccan.

Palas :

The Palas patronised several Sanskrit scholars, some of whom were their officials. Many Buddhist Tantric works were written and translated during the Pala rule. Besides the Buddhist scholars already mentioned, Jimutavahana, Sandhyakar Nandi, Madhava-kara, Suresvara and Chakrapani Datta are some of the other notable scholars during this period. Pala texts on philosophy include 'Agama Shastra' by Gaudapada, 'Nyaya Kundali' by Sridhar Bhatta and 'Karmanushthan Paddhati' by Bhatta Bhavadeva. The writings on medicine include

(i) 'Chikitsa Samgraha', 'Ayurveda Dipika', 'Bhanumati', 'Shabda Chandrika' and 'Dravya Gunasangraha' by Chakrapani Datta
(ii) Shabda-Pradipa, Vrikkhayurveda and Lohpaddhati by Sureshwara
(iii) Chikitsa Sarsamgraha by Vangasena
(iv) Sushrata by Gadadhara Vaidya
(v) Dayabhaga, Vyavohara Matrika and Kalaviveka by Jimutavahana

Sandhyakar Nandi's Ramacharitam (12th century) is an important source of Pala history. A type of the proto-Bengali language can be observed in the Charyapadas composed during the Pala rule.

4.3.2 Religion

The Chalukyas were the followers of Brahmanical religion and no wonder Buddhism began to decline. However they followed a policy of religious toleration. During their ascendancy, Jainism prospered in the Deccan. There is nothing to show that Buddhism was also patronised by the Chalukya rulers. Buddhism might have been on the decline but it had not became out. As regards Brahmanism the Pauranic deities rose into prominence. Superb structures were set up at Badami and Pattadakal in respect of Brahma, Vishnu and Siva. The sacrificial form of worship received special attention. Pulakesin I alone is stated to have performed a number of sacrifices such as Vajapeya, Asvamedha, Paundarika etc. The great religious reform which swept India in the 8th century first originated in the Pallava kingdom. The Vaishnava and Saiva literature of the Tamils mainly developed during this period. The Vaishnava and Saiva saints whose lives and words dominate the religion of the south lived during the Pallava period. The Jain and Buddhist teachers slowly lost their place. The Pallavas were the followers of Brahmanism and therefore Brahmanism was acclaimed as the. The state religion. Pallavas were mostly the followers of Vishnu but sometimes they were the devotees of Siva. They got constructed a number of temples. It is the Pallavas who set the base of the great reformation which took place in the 8th century. During the Pallava rule the Aryanisation of South India was completed.

In the Pallava territory the Dharamsutras had gained dominance. The university of Kanchi have played on important role in this connection. It was from Kanchi that the Sanskritistation of the south and the Indian colonies in the far east proceeded. Rashtrakutas rulers not only patronised Saivism and Vaishnavism but also protected Jainism, Buddhism and Islâm. They permitted the Muslim merchants to settle in their kingdom, build mosques and preach their religion. Their tolerant policies gave great impetus to trade and commerce. Pala rulers were great patrons of Buddhist learning and religion. Dharmapala founded the famous Buddhist monastery at Vikramashila. During Palas time the fame of Nalanda University spread all over the world. Nalada had more than 10,000 students and teachers coming not only from various regions of India but also from China, Sri Lanka, Central Asia. The University imparted education in different branches of knowledge. Devapala donated income from five villages to support Nalanda University. The Pala kings patronised Hinduism too. They gave donations for living and educational purpose. Vinayakapala the Pala king built one thousand temples in respect of the Saiva deity. They gave donations to Brahmans to settle down in their country and run gurukulas.

The Pratihara kings were followers of Hindusim. They beautiful Kanauj with many fine temples and building. The building of temples and the educational institutions attached with them formed community projects in which the entire village citizens participated. For this object they made contributions both in cash and kinds regardless of their occupation.

4.3.3 Art and Architecture

Art made tremendous progress under the patronage of Chalukya kings. A new style of architecture known as the Chalukya style was developed during this period. At Aihole alone we come across 70 temples. Along with Aihole there were temple at Badami and Pattadakal. Aihole represents the best of Chalukyan architecture. During the seventh century A.D. that the movement of rock cut halls was initiated. The temple of Virupaksha at Pattadakal is the most important one. It was built by Lokamahadevi the queen of Vikramaditya II. It has many features similar to those of the Kailashnath temple at Kanchi. Another queen of Vikramaditya II constructed another great temple of Siva under the name of Trailokesvara in the vicinity of the Virupaksha temple. Mangalesa the early chalukya king got excavated at Badami a beautiful cave temple of Siva. Vijayaditya another Chalukya built the great temple of Siva known as Sangamesvara at Pattadakal in Bijapur district. His sister built a Jain temple called Anesejjeyabasadi at Lakshmeswar. Under the Pallavas art and architecture witnessed great progress. The Pallavas got constructed a number of temple. The temple architecture of the Pallavas can be divided into two categories viz rock cut and structural. During the time of Pallava king Mahendravarman I the practive of scooping entire temples out of solid rock was introduced of which the rathas of Mahabalipuram are fine examples. During the reign of Narasimhavarman II the remarkable architectural activities which initiated a particular style popularly known as the Dravidian style of temple architecture was introduced. The Mukteshwara and Matungeshwara temples at Kanchi, Persurameshwara temple at Gudimallan and Vedamallisavara temple at Oragadam belong to the pallava period. It cannot be denied that the credit of initiating a movement in temple architecture belongs to the Pallavas.

During the pandya time architecture. There are groups of small temples at Tiruchirappalli in Tamil Nadu. The Shiva temples have a Nandi bull in front of the maha mandapa. Finely sculptured idols, gopurams on the vimanas were developed. Meenakshi Amman Temple in Madurai and Nellaiappar Temple in Tirunelveli were built during the reign of the Pandyas.

The Rashtrakutas made a magnificent contribution to Indian art. Their rock - cut cave temples excavated at Ellora belonging to Brahmanical, Buddhist and Jain faiths are the symbols of their religious toleration and are one of the splendours of Indian arts. The famous rock cut Shiva temple at Ellora which is justly regarded as a marvel of architecture was constructed under the order of Rashtrakuta King Krishna I and bears an eloquent tesimony to the high level of skill attained by India in the art of sculpture and architecture. It is unfortunate that no buildings of the Pala period are in existence.

✧ EXERCISE ✧

Q. I : Write the answers of the following questions in 100 words.

1. Why did Pulakesin I is regarded as the first great king among the Chalukya rulers ?
2. Explain the achievements of Vikramaditya I of Chalukyan king.
3. Give an account of the Pallava king Narsimhavarman II.
4. Why did Varguna I is known as the greatest imperialist of Pallava dynasty.
5. Explain the role of Dantivarman as the founder of Rashtrakuta dynasty.
6. Estimate the countribution of Devapala in the Pala dynasty.

Q. II : Give the answers of the following questions in 300 words.

1. Discuss the role of Maharaja Kirtivarman I in the Chalukya dynasty.
2. Explain the role of Nandivarman II of Pallava dynasty.

3. What is the contribution of the Rashtrakuta king Amoghavarsha I ?
4. Give an account of the achievements of the Rashtrakuta king India III.

Q. 3 : Give the answers of the following questions in 500 words.

1. Why did Pulakesin II was known as the greatest rulers among the Chalukya dynasty ?
2. Why did Narsimhavarman I was identified as the most powerful ruler of Pallava dynasty ?
3. Discuss the struggle between the Chalukyas, Pallavas and Pandyas over supremacy for the Peninsular India ?
4. Why did the Pala king Dharmapala is known as the man of dynamitic personality ?

Q. 4 : Write short notes on the following.

1. Vinayaditya of Chalukya dynasty.
2. Narsimhavarman II of Pallava dynasty.
3. Krishna I of Rashtrakuta dynasty.
4. Ramapala of Pala dynasty.

✧ BIBLIOGRAPHY ✧

1. Thapar Romila : Early India : From the Origins to A.D. 1300 Penguin Books, 2002.
2. Sharma R.S. : Rethinking India is past, Oxford University press New Delhi, 2009.
3. Basham A.L. : The Wonder that was India, Picador - Pan Macmillan, Reprinted 2004.
4. Mujumdar R.C. : 'Ancient India' Motilal Banarsidas Publishers Varanasi 1952.
5. Mahajan V.D. : Ancient India S. Chand and Company Ltd. New Delhi. Reprinted 2019.

✿ ✿ ✿

F.Y.B.A. (Semester - II)

HISTORY

G1-Early India : Post Mauryan Age to the Rashtrakutas
(2019 Pattern)

Time : 2 ½ **Hours** **Max. Marks : 70**

Instructions to the candidates :

1. All questions are compulsory.
2. Figures to the right indicates full marks.

Q. 1 : Answer the following questions in 300 words. (any one) **[15]**

(a) Explain the role of Pushyamitra Sunga in the Sunga dynasty.

OR

(b) Discuss the social conditions during the Gupta Period ?

Q. 2 : Answer the following questions in 300 words. (any one) **[15]**

(a) What is the achievement of the Cheras during the Sangam age ?

OR

(b) What is the contribution of the Rashtrakuta king Amoghavarsha I ?

Q. 3 : Answer the following questions in 200 words. (any two). **[20]**

(a) Give the account of the Shakas king.

(b) Explain the contribution of the Cholas during the period of Sangam Literature ?

(c) Chandragupta I as the founder of the Gupta empire ?

(d) Discuss the achievements of the Rashtrakuta king Dantivarman of Dantidurga ?

Q. 4 : Short notes. (any four) **[20]**

(a) Gandhara school of Art.

(b) Pandya king Nedunjeliyan.

(c) Nalanda University.

(d) Rampala of Pala dynasty.

(e) Sri Yajna Satakarni.

(f) Krishna I Rashtrakuta dynasty ?

✿ ✿ ✿